OIKOS: God's Big Word for a Small Planet

OIKOS
God's Big Word for a Small Planet

A Theology of
Economy, Ecology, and Ecumeny

ANDREW FRANCIS

 CASCADE *Books* · Eugene, Oregon

OIKOS
God's Big Word for a Small Planet

Cascade Books
An Imprint of Wipf and Stock Publishers
199 W. 8th Ave., Suite 3
Eugene, OR 97401

www.wipfandstock.com

PAPERBACK ISBN: 978-1-4982-3517-4
HARDCOVER ISBN: 978-1-4982-3519-8
EBOOK ISBN: 978-1-4982-3518-1

Cataloguing-in-Publication data:

Names: Francis, Andrew.
Title: Oikos : God's big word for a small planet / Andrew Francis.
Description: Eugene, OR: Cascade Books, 2017 | Includes bibliographical references.
Identifiers: ISBN 978-1-4982-3517-4 (paperback) | ISBN 978-1-4982-3519-8 (hardcover) | ISBN 978-1-4982-3518-1 (ebook)
Subjects: LCSH: 1. Environmental economics. | 2. Sustainable development. I. Title.
Classification: HC79.E5 F696 2017 (print) | HC79 (ebook)

Manufactured in the U.S.A.   APRIL 19, 2017

This is book is dedicated to three sets of folks, who ensure my vision and thinking takes account of the world in which we live.

First, for my "brothers in alms", whose generosity of heart, mind, and pocket have enriched my life:

      Allan Armstrong
          Stuart Hodby
              David Nash
                    Jeremy Thomson

and second their wives, respectively: Gloria, Stephanie, Sally, and Kathy.

Finally, for the next generation of my family, as they set out in the world:

      Caroline Heath
          Nicholas Hodby
              Philip Hodby
                  Sophie Hodby
                      Angharad Nash

"Every part of the earth is sacred to my people . . . our God is also your God: the earth is precious to him and to harm the world is to heap contempt upon its creator . . . this we know; the earth does not belong to man, man belongs to the earth".

– CHIEF SEATTLE

"I have come that they may have life—life in all its fullness".

– JESUS OF NAZARETH

"The roots of ecology, economics and ecumenism are all in *oikos*: with the right management of the [global] household—respect for the integrity of nature and equitable sharing of resources—all can be included at the dinner table".

– SALLIE MCFAGUE

Contents

Acknowledgements

This book owes its genesis to my life's journey through so many countries and communities, and with good *compañeros*—I have been blessed by God in every one of them.

Without our family's ophthalmologist, Peter Rocket, and my gifted cataract surgeon, Thamir Yasen, I would have lost so much of my sight while this book was being written, and would have given my library away, and you would have had only a tiny bibliography. But without my high school wrestling with E. F. Schumacher and Peter Kropotkin, and the biblical prophets and the Gospels about Jesus of Nazareth, I would not have begun to see the world as I have come to understand it.

Without my mother's and father's encouragement, I would not have traveled or learned to make multidisciplinary connections about life, the universe, and everything that impacts the communities in which we live.

But my "brothers in alms" and their wives keep me challenging my own lifestyle and learning, asking the big and detailed questions which develop the "currency of ideas." It is also the hope and conversation of my close family's next generation, now wrestling with their university studies and first jobs, that inspire me to dedicate this book to them, too.

So it is thanks to both James Stock and Robin Parry, at Wipf and Stock, who recognized the potential for and supported the publication of this book. Thanks to Rodney Clapp, my wise and patient editor there, all the backroom team, Mike Surber for the great cover, and their publicity crew for ensuring you hold this book in your hands. Thank you to you for (buying and) reading it.

Without the support and critique of many friends, this book would not have made it this far. My thanks go to Allan Armstrong, Ollie Henshall, Sarah Lane Cawte, Poppy Leeder, Annie J. Peters, Paul Sunners, and Jeremy

Thomson, who all read extracts or discussed the trajectories of the text as it was being brought together. I owe many thanks to Trisha Dale for pulling the text into Chicago style shape. Thank you also to Alastair McIntosh and Stuart Masters for the back cover commendations.

Finally, I can never give nor show enough gratitude to my loving partner, Janice Hodby. She shares my "take" on the world, our home, and mutual joy in hospitality, as we welcome friend and stranger. Whether in that welcoming, or cultivating our garden, or just watching the sunset, Janice patiently inspires me to write day after day.

About the writer

Andrew Francis is a UK-based community theologian as well as a published writer and poet. He now focuses much of his other public ministry as a conference speaker, seminar leader, and Christian preacher.

After early studies in law and theology, he went on to gain an MTh for his thesis on radical Christian communities, resulting in *Anabaptism: Radical Christianity* (2011). Later, he studied for his doctorate at Princeton Theological Seminary. His dissertation there explored the Christian use of hospitality and shared food; this was published in a UK popular version: *Hospitality and Community After Christendom* (2012). Until cardiac illness intervened, he served for nearly thirty years as a congregationally based United Reformed Church pastor, in the UK and France.

He has also served the wider church as an adult educator and group accompanier as well as working for the BBC as a broadcaster and religious programs editor. He oversaw the building and early development of a French retreat house. He was the UK's first Anabaptist Network development worker and formerly was vice-chair of the UK's Mennonite Trust.

His social policy writing includes his previous Cascade book, *What in God's Name Are You Eating?* (2014), about food ethics, and the multi-authored *Foxes Have Holes: Reflections upon Britain's Housing Need* (2016), which he edited. A biographical study of a theologian, *Dorothee Soelle: Life and Work* (2015), is to be followed by one of English writer Lawrence Durrell in 2019. His other theological work includes *Shalom: The Jesus Manifesto* (2016), an in-production theology of mission for 2018, and a future liturgical/pastoral theology volume.

A former potter and artist, he is a joyful cook and jam-maker, enjoying growing food in his community garden. He lives in southwest England. His personal website is www.anmchara.com; *anmchara* is Gaelic for "soul friend."

Introduction

I begin with two stories from the opposite poles of planet Earth. First, the Nenet caribou[1] herders of the Siberian Arctic peninsula of Yamal are among the last surviving racial subgroups of nomads anywhere in the world. The Yamal is home to the largest number of caribou on the planet and they are "managed" by the 15,000-strong Nenet people.

Working in small groups of two to five tent-dwelling families, they follow the centuries-old traditional cycle of taking their caribou north for the summer, where the animals graze on the exposed tundra. The people and their herds move south for the winter so that the caribou can dig into and feed upon snow-covered lichens. The Nenet retain animist beliefs that all their world and its component parts—animal, vegetable, earth, and human—are inextricably bound together as a "spiritual" whole. But both their world and worldviews are threatened.

The Yamal is one enormous gas field and is now being exploited in its commercial development by the Russian conglomerate GazProm, bringing the railroad, settlements, and roadways to the region. Now, each Nenet family receives a monthly $30/£20 allowance from the state to help them meet the necessary costs of encounters with twenty-first-century materialism. One hangover of the old Soviet system is that all Nenet children must now go away for state boarding school education for at least ten years from the age of seven; many Nenet teenagers fail to grow up learning the traditional crafts and skills to maintain their culture's nomadic lifestyle.

In 2013, global warming was acknowledged to have led to a winter thaw then refreeze, which resulted in the starvation and death of over 15,000 caribou and thus sixty families lost their livelihoods. They became wage-slaves and predominantly slaughtermen, killing their remaining and

1. Caribou are called reindeer in English-speaking Europe and Australia.

other caribou to help feed the railroad staff, construction teams, and gas workers. Now the number of caribou is not being viably sustained, because of those growing human demands, so a vicious cycle of potentially terminal decline has begun for both Yamal's caribou and the traditional Nenet way of life.

Second, in the Antarctic's oceans, a battle is raging. Each year, the Japanese whaling fleet is challenged by the ships, helicopters, and tactics of the international marine wildlife conservation organization, Sea Shepherd,[2] to prevent the further killing of whales. My views about the consumption of whale meat and personal objections to the hunting of whales are already documented.[3] The publication and broadcast of my two-voice graphic poem about the demise of a South Atlantic whaling station are in the public domain.[4] My commitment to peacemaking and nonviolent action[5] makes me question the more extreme tactics of Sea Shepherd's fleet.

Having seen orcas from the Orkney ferry and minkes off the Irish coast, I love whales and their graceful *joie de vivre* as they swim wild as God intended. They are gentle creatures, although the adjective is relative when considering the courtship rituals of the larger species (which weigh many times more than yellow school buses!). Most whales feed on plankton or krill and even the alpha predator orcas have never been documented as deliberately killing humans in the wild (in marked contrast to captive orcas[6]). Why do allegedly civilized nations, like Japan or Iceland, persist in the hunting of increasingly endangered whales? How many Japanese or Icelandic consumers have witnessed the innate cruelty of harpooning a live, unanesthetized giant of the sea and dragging it to a slow death by drowning?

Despite the International Court of Justice ruling in 2014 that Japanese whaling is illegal and must stop, the Japanese declared in late 2015 that they would resume limited whaling in 2016; as we go to press this saga continues. There are sustainable alternative sources of marine protein. No wonder acquaintances who support Sea Shepherd have challenged me to be a volunteer for the internationally staffed Antarctic fleet; regrettably, my

2. www.seashepherd.org.

3. Francis, *What in God's Name*, 108–10.

4. Francis, *Earth, Air, Fire, Water*, 75.

5. Francis, *Shalom*, 138–48.

6. Kirby, *Death at Sea World*.

life-limiting heart condition means I could not even pass the medical to be a ship's cook.

Both of these narratives describe learning journeys. Each year the Nenet find that ancient migratory herd-ways are now blocked by new rail-track or road embankments. Although most Sea Shepherd volunteers are white, westernized, and well-educated, they are also of all creeds or none and learned about the plight of whales, making considered choices to risk their lives to "save the whales." In today's world, as the hunt for resources strengthens in the face of human need, we all have to do three things:

1. Recognize the plight of the planet for both human and other species.
2. Learn about the cost of making changes for the benefit of all.
3. Decide how much commitment each of us will make to ensure those changes occur—whatever the cost.

As the economist Robert Costanza summarizes: "Probably the most challenging task facing humanity today is the creation of a shared vision of a sustainable and desirable society, one that can provide permanent prosperity within the biophysical constraints of the real world in a way that is fair and equitable to all of humanity, to other species and to future generations."[7]

It is relatively simple to see how this can apply to caribou, Yamal, and the Nenet or whaling in the southern oceans. Yet between the poles is literally a world of similar tensions perhaps not so easily identifiable nor solvable. Theologian Sallie McFague personalizes the cost of Costanza's vision: "The route to it, however, for folks like me and you . . . involves limitation and sacrifice, a radically different view of abundance. It involves re-imagining the good life in just and sustainable ways."[8] If the Nenet, their caribou, or Antarctic whales are to have a future, we must learn to see ourselves as part of that shared future, too.

Oikos means "household"

The interconnectedness of planetary life is masked by westernized consumerism and lifestyles. Would GazProm in their commercial search for

7. Costanza, ed., *Introduction to Ecological Economics*, 179.
8. McFague, *Life Abundant*, xii.

profit welcome the global community's intervention to protect the Nenet people and the caribou? However, the increasing moral support for the Sea Shepherd organization demonstrates that globally people are prepared to object when westernized consumerism goes too far. Over some time, without baleen whales, the exponential growth of krill will ultimately clog up the oceans, just as effectively as a chemical pollutant. Hunting whales to extinction engenders geo-suicide.

We have to make connections. That "we" means people like you and me who have both time and education to read books, to explore the issues, and to act both politically and economically for change. In my lifetime, we have seen the growth of the multinational (a.k.a. transnational) corporation, whose economic powers transcend those of single nations and whose political might can overcome community protest or ecological concerns. A relatively neutral example is that (as I write) World Bank statistics identify that the gross turnover of Coca-Cola is greater than the gross national product of all but four African nations and the majority of European Union countries.

We now live in a global community. No longer can we consider our own nation as its own household. There are at least as big if not bigger transnationals, whose economic priorities can (and often do) override the best interests of our own nation. We have to learn to live as part of a new global community, in which decisions taken in one region can have repercussions around the world. The global financial crash of 2008 is often attributed to Japan as its source by those who would prefer to divert attention from the overselling of subprime mortgages in North America or a too-rapid fiscal expansion of the European Union. We are in this together—but what we should note is that all these contributory factors took place in westernized, northern hemisphere regions. Westernized Australasia may have been implicated in the recession but was not to blame for the crash. But what is more frightening is to realize that one billion-plus nations of India and China also cannot be held responsible for the 2008 crash. Neither can the poorer southern hemisphere nations, meaning that over half the world's peoples had no say in what could destroy their economies. They have no real control over the north's effects upon them. It is as though the prophetic challenge of the 1980 Brandt Report[9] never happened.

There is a helpful Greek word, *oikos*, which means either "house" or "household" depending upon its attendant verbs or adjectives. It is from

9. Brandt, ed., *North-South*.

this Greek root that English speakers gain three important words: "eco-nomical," "ecological," and "ecumenical." Those words gain an even more "life-giving" significance when considering the future of our planet. The interrelationship of economic, ecological, and ecumenical factors help us reflect upon, then ask, the necessary questions needed to act decisively and live together for the sake of this single small planet.

Christians and those from other faith communities have a distinct worldview, which is neither nihilist nor fatalistic but realistic about the fu-ture. We have to acknowledge that particularly non-believers but often our-selves find it hard to accept that "God envisions church and world as they currently are not."[10] More about the church, later. For now—if the classical "faith views" of God can be accepted as a premise—then that same God has a purpose for the creation, which does not mean its self-destruction but a different culmination. The Bible repeatedly uses the word *oikos* in its expansion of the divine purpose for the world.

A Small Planet?

The contracts for this book were signed just weeks before NASA's planet-hunting spacecraft, *Kepler*, had located a "cousin" to Earth, now called Ke-pler 425b. This new (to us) planet is in the Cygnus constellation, some 1,400 light years away from Earth. Kepler 425b is what is known as an exo-planet, which circles a "sun-like star" in 385 days—similar to Earth's orbit of 365 days. Kepler 425b is about one and a half times the size of Earth, giving it a mass of five times Earth's. These facts place it in the "Goldilocks zone," meaning Kepler 425b may be inhabitable (and even inhabited), sustaining surface water and equable temperatures, if its surface is rocky (scientific projection suggests 60 percent probability), rather than a "gaseous surface," like Neptune. Neither I nor my publishers claim any monopoly on pro-phetic wisdom, but the very presence of such a world as Kepler 425b does mean that Earth is truly the "Small Planet" of this book's subtitle.

The ecology of this "new" planet will take generations, if not light years, to discover. Whether we as homo sapiens ever get that opportunity will be determined by our survival beyond mere subsistence existence. What it will take will be globally shared priorities both economically and ecumenically if ecologically wise policies are to prevail to ensure humanity does not curtail planet Earth's future. Philosophers may take a *que sera sera*

10. Brueggemann, *Living toward a Vision*, 40.

approach, accepting global annihilation or mutually assured destruction or survival with a logical, even reasoned equanimity. However theologians, of whatever faith, must argue from a Godward dimension.

As this book goes into its final production phase, in September 2016, Harvard University sources confirmed the existence of another large planet, Proxima b, close to Proxima Centauri, which also has the capability to sustain human life. During all this, scientific confirmation of the existence of "running water" on Mars continues to beg the question, "Is there life on Mars?" Scientific investigation of Kepler 425b, Proxima b, and Mars reminds us that Earth is still a small planet in comparison to these others.

God's big word

To understand that economical, ecological, and ecumenical interrelationship, as a theologian and/or as a Christian disciple or simply an inquisitive bystander, means that *all* the developing debate can have a Godward dimension. God's *oikos* vision in the Bible is of Earth as a "household." In our homes, to live harmoniously within our means, we must live within our economic constraints, within the nature and sustaining of our neighborhood's environment, sharing peaceably with the human community around us. Why should that set of constraints and questions be any different, except in scale, when we consider what it means to live in this part of God's household—Earth? Therefore *oikos* is God's big word for a small planet.

God's purpose for humanity is to share fully in creation together. The biblical allegories of creation in Genesis, with the placing of humanity in the garden of Eden (Gen 2) were just that. Adam wrecked that by taking the apple from Eve. When ongoing humanity failed to live "ecumenically" with one another, many Middle Eastern narratives tell of a divinely inspired flood in the Tigris-Euphrates valley to prophetically begin again good living together within creation.[11] The story of Joseph's interpretation of Pharaoh's dream tells of both stewardship and "economic" planning so that resources could be justly shared in future days of famine, drought, and privation. God's invitation to the Hebrews to accept wilderness wandering was on the basis that future generations, forty years hence, would enjoy "a land flowing with milk and honey." For many contemporary Jewish believers, the promises of God, their praise in the Psalms and the biblical prophets

11. Francis, *Shalom*, 19.

of past centuries, found their fulfilment in the 1948 creation of the state of Israel—the promised homeland—*oikos* within God's creation. When I have been a guest of Galilean *kibbutzim*, having been well fed on homegrown vegetables and local lamb, sitting in good company, drinking local arak as the sun went down, this betokened a Jewish theology of *oikos*—dwelling well within God's creation.

I recently edited a book about UK housing, in which I used the life and teaching of Jesus to help readers construct a coherent theology of housing.[12] We need only think of Jesus' encounter with Zacchaeus or Peter's mother-in-law or Lazarus, Martha, and Mary, or consider the Parables of the Good Samaritan and the Prodigal Son, to realize how important "dwelling well" within God's creation is for Jesus, and his ministry and mission. The Christian New Testament is woven through with both greetings and references to household ministries. The Greek-language New Testament uses *oikos* 114 times with its differing emphases; fifty-five of those instances are within Luke-Acts, which majors upon the "household" imagery surrounding God's people and their Jesus-shaped mission. *Oikos* must be at the heart of every reasoned Christian theology if it was so much a part of Jesus' life and legacy.

As a radical Christian from the Anabaptist tradition, I believe Jesus' life and teaching provide the exemplar for all human discipleship—both individually and in community.[13] I have had a blessed life journey, visiting four continents of Earth, have never been homeless or starving, spending half of my life as a Christian pastor working within communities and local neighborhoods for change. Some of the detailed theology of that Jesus-ethic, green politics, and lifestyle changes will become apparent in the coming pages. But all these have gradually contributed to an *oikos* theology—that God is calling *all* people to live within a new economic order and ecological lifestyle for the sake of the planet and for *all* my sisters and brothers who share life upon it, both now and in the future. As I have preached on Sundays and led conferences or seminars, I have increasingly understood that *oikos* is God's big word to and for a small planet.

12. Francis, *Foxes Have Holes*, 103–11.
13. Francis, *Shalom*.

Rethinking the future . . .

A theology of *oikos* is a coherent framework for presenting afresh a global ethic for the interrelationship between economy, ecology, and ecumenism. Amplifying my previous McFague quotation:

> The issues are global, systemic, economic and political: hence the solutions must be as well. An ecological liberation theology will involve at least two such tasks. One is envisioning an alternative good life, and the other is working to make systemic changes, especially economic ones, so that this alternative vision can have a public impact. The alternative notion of the abundant life would be radically different from the current 'good life' from which most of us benefit.[14]

This *oikos* book represents a lifetime of praxis, both action and reflection, upon such *oikos* thinking, inevitably challenging our westernized views and comforts as McFague's quote predicts we should.

What lies ahead are three topic-focused sections—"Economy," "Ecology," and "Ecumeny"[15]—before a concluding three-part section, which attempts through both biography and practical advocacy to demonstrate making such *oikos* a prophetic reality now. Each of those three topic-focused sections contain their own three chapters: one explores the subject, another explores humanity's predilection to its abuse, while each section's final chapter offers some alternative Godward patterns of that topic's daily expression. Within all the analysis and advocacy is the God-talk about it, enabling us to weave new patterns of theology to speak into the world's debates as Earth's crises deepen for all its peoples.

As the central focus is to make the unifying *oikos* link, I can only paint the broad brushstrokes of each part of this triptych. Other than the narratives offered and the geographical examples provided, much of the detail and pointillistic moments for you will be provided by your experience, reading, and context.

---

14. McFague, *Life Abundant*, 35.

15. I have deliberately kept the word "ecumeny" rather than the better known adjective "ecumenical." I first encountered the frequent use of the word "ecumeny," as a noun meaning "those who are ecumenical" or more loosely "the outward looking (religious) community," amongst English- and German-speaking Lutherans. The term was frequently used at the annual German *Kirchentag*, a city-wide ecumenical festival of lectures, seminars, worship, and other gatherings.

Some years ago, the zoologist John Walsh led the rescue of animals trapped or abandoned by the rising waters behind Surinam's newly built Afobaka dam. He recounted his experiences in his book, *Time is Short and the Water Rises*.[16] The economic and ecological waters respectively threaten to drown our planet metaphorically and literally, as ecumenically more of God's people live at odds with both one another—whether poor or rich, of faith or not—and with our fellow species. No longer is this just about Antarctic whales or the Nenet and their caribou. It is about the agenda of the world between them, too. "*Time is Short . . .*" means it is time to read on . . .

16. Walsh and Gannon, *Time is Short*.

ECONOMY

1 Render to Caesar?

They say, "See Venice—and die!" I nearly did—but that is a story for later.

Historically, Venice virtually sat at the crossroads of the trade routes from China and the rest of Asia, across to Africa, through the Mediterranean, and up into Europe. Because of late-medieval, regional, internecine violence, folks escaped into the shallow Venetian lagoon area, building houses, quays, and market spaces on pilings driven into the sandy or clay banks, hidden just below the surface. It grew to be the world's greatest trading city.

For half a millennium, the Venetian ducat was the basis of gold currency: it was not two centuries ago that a ducat would buy a closet of fine clothes or a feast for family and friends or a night with the best courtesan. But as in so many rich societies, the laboring poor had been kept in order with a daily evening meal and tiny wages. Those who managed workers had part of their wages paid in easily dried *sale* (sea-salt), giving rise to their payments being known as *salare*, hence "salary." That pure sea salt was a sought-after commodity, its production being controlled by the doge (Venetian ruler) and the merchants, who traded in ducats. Those with just a *salare* could use their salt to trade with the city's restaurants, shopkeepers, local fisherman, and the vegetable sellers who came across the lagoon by boat.

Venice was a mercantile trading economy, where the richest could fund explorers such as Marco Polo or the captains of ships from other nations, who subsequently discovered the Americas and East Indies.[1] Venice provided a prophetic microcosm of currency trading at different levels.

Learning from my past

As elementary schoolboys with a few pennies each week, we bought bubble gum whose unique selling point was the enclosed, facsimile, historic US bank notes. The phase lasted about a year as weekly, we accrued more "wealth"; occasionally, you might get a $10 or $100 bill, among the more usual early greenbacks. Boys from a neighboring housing project preferred to trade and keep Confederate (not really understanding the politics) to the Union notes my group preferred. There were more of those Confederate collectors, so our bartering power increased—we would give only three Confederate dollars away in return for five Union ones. We began trading other things, like pens and pocket knives, for these mock dollars and, in our childish ways, we were learning lessons "about the way the world worked."

From the Norman Conquest in 1066, England developed an administrative class separate from the clergy, but increasingly a social hierarchy that rewarded those loyal to the crown with land, wealth, title, and rule over the populace. Deep in English history, we know that the peasant class had subsistence lives without money, living in hovels, scratching a living from the land with occasional handouts from the lord of the manor in return for their agricultural labor and soldiering. People were kept in check by the supply of food. Just like my contemporaries with our bubble gum bank notes, folk learned to trade, with some becoming wealthy and selling either the products of their land or their skills in local markets. What began as a barter economy grew as cities minted their own currencies, while the lords of each manor accrued gold—in similar fashion to Venetians and their ducats. No wonder folklore developed their heroes, such as Robert the Bruce in Scotland or the mythical Robin Hood[2] who "robbed the rich and gave to the poor" in England.

It was traders from Italy (e.g., the Lombards) or itinerant Jewish moneylenders, such as Shakespeare's Shylock in *The Merchant of Venice*, who began organizing promissory notes between differently located branches of their family. So someone could pay in gold in one country, traveling home in relative safety and redeeming their wealth later. By 1600, there was a

1. da Mosto, *Francesco's Venice*.
2. *Robin Hood: Prince of Thieves*, 1991 film/DVD, dir. Kevin Reynolds.

well-established international economy. This was reflected in patterns of trade, the support of exploration and of such international "banking."

Britain's Industrial Revolution changed society from an agrarian and market-town economy. Workers flocked to fast-growing cities to work in mills and factories, the majority living in rapidly erected, poor-quality housing, often rented from the factory owners.[3] But the UK needed successive legislation from 1725, known as the Truck Acts, outlawing the "company store" system, which effectively put company workers into debt bondage (i.e., slavery), creating company-defined "closed economies." In similar ways, the trading post in US frontier towns, beloved of B-movie Westerns, operated similarly closed economies because they were the only local point of trade. North American economies are predicated upon the breaking out from the mix of the trading post and the barter economy of the first settlers.[4]

Britain was colonizing the world, as well as trading with it, leaching seemingly unending products for their domestic markets from all corners of its world.[5] Quite fairly, the more organized and wealthier colonies objected to the UK's imposition of taxation upon them, arguing "no taxation without representation." The prime example is the iconic 1773 Boston Tea Party, when Britain's violent reaction precipitated the American Revolution. The empire was indeed fighting back and the modern era of economics had begun.

Almost simultaneously with this, the Scots philosopher and polymath Adam Smith (1723–90) was writing *The Wealth of Nations*,[6] which became foundational, leading to Smith being described as "the father of modern economics." I first read Smith nearly forty years ago when I spent five years (before seminary) working for a regional unit of the UK's national industrial relations/mediation organization, ACAS.[7] There, several of the "fast-trackers" were informally tutored by a senior colleague, an Oxford economics graduate, through a reading program to understand the economic world and strategies that underpinned our daily work. Just as then, if we are now to analyze economic ills and advocate alternatives, we must do the same and learn something of the development of economic theory.

3. Thomson, *Making of the English Working Class*, 352.
4. Hart, *Trading Nation*.
5. Keay, *Honourable Company*.
6. Smith, *Wealth of Nations*.
7. www.acas.org.uk

Learning from economic theory

The jury remains out on Adam Smith. There are those who believe *The Wealth of Nations* is intentionally theological, with the social order built upon the concept of God acting within nature; others view him as skeptically deistic, because he never explicitly mentions God. Classical economists argue that Smith's "wealth of nations" concept is supreme, promoting a "free market economy," effectively dog-eat-dog, when only the most competitive will survive. Neoclassical economists emphasize Smith's "invisible hand" concept, which presumes that when an individual acts in their best self-interest, it will benefit the whole society. However the faces of those spinning coins fall for you, Smith is still important because he mapped out the ground for economic discussion, while also stating:

- The existence of obvious inequalities in bargaining power between workers and masters (capital holders);

- That wages cannot be statutorily regulated because different market forces—such as supply and demand of labor—occur;

- That all "subjects" should contribute towards the upkeep of the state, thus advocating progressive personal taxation and not just taxes upon goods and services.

Alfred Marshall (1842–1924) is our next key player as his book *Principles of Economics*[8] critiqued Smith and others, but drew together a threefold woven cord of cohering theory. First, he reaffirmed the principle of supply and demand, particularly for labor and goods (including natural resources). Second, he realized the need to pass on the "costs of production" to the consumer or buyer. Third, he recognized that the consumption or use of either a "service" or an item may increase or decrease as a second or subsequent such unit is purchased; this is known as the "marginal utility cost." Alongside this Marshall delineated an ongoing principle of economic geography, known as "Marshall industrialization," showing that industries become most profitable if those of the same type are geographically colocated, thus able to utilize local natural resources or the pool of skilled labor. Marshall's *Principles* became *the* standard textbook for decades to come.

Western society was rapidly changing, from and around that First World War era. So-called *laissez-faire* economics, akin to Smith's classical dog-eat-dog position, saying let the market decide who survives, was the

8. Marshall, *Principles of Economics.*

favored model of the rich and/or politically powerful. During the 1920s boom, most Western governments agreed to link their currency rates (e.g., the US$–UK£ rate) to the price of gold, effectively tying their own currency to a particular value while also agreeing not to print more money than for which they had hard gold equivalence. This became known as "the gold standard," creating a federalized money system without political union (akin to today's Eurozone)—a voluntary straitjacket.

One of Marshall's Cambridge students was John Maynard Keynes (1883–1946), who was part of London's "Bloomsbury set." Despite critique and counterpoint theories, Keynesian economics are still important today for their influence upon the development of twentieth-century capitalism. Basically, Keynes argued for clear, direct state intervention to moderate the effects of so-called boom-and-bust economies. Keynes challenged the neoclassical view that that in a "free market economy" there can always be full employment providing that all workers are flexible both in their wage rates and demands. I would simply question whether such neoclassical advocates can morally accept the consequent poverty of the lowest paid workers' families.[9]

Keynesians needed to, and did, provide a strong working model for the West, in marked contrast to the rise of the "communist system" of economics and state control, so evident in post-Revolution Russia and other Soviet republics. What non-economists often fail to appreciate is the breadth and depth of Karl Marx's comprehensive analysis of capitalism,[10] yet how cursory is his initial advocacy of communist-style political systems. A key concept in Marx's thinking was "value."

- Was a worker paid a proper value for their labor, or were they just paid the minimum necessary for survival?

- Was the value of a commodity recognized? E.g., food had huge human and market value whereas money had only metallic value as gold or silver and paper money should be regarded as simply state promissory notes (with little real value!).

- How the mode of production created fresh "value," dependent upon both the product (e.g., coal, clothes, etc) with direct benefits for people or "labor" when the productive workers may actually need far more

9. Keynes, *Essential Keynes.*
10. Marx, *Capital.*

practical skill than the overseers just shouting at them to produce more.

Marx (1818–83) became a penniless German émigré, finally arriving in England where his writing, life, and family were supported by a philanthropic Manchester factory manager, Friedrich Engels (1820–95), who had been appalled by the social conditions that he was witnessing.[11] Engels believed the world needed Marxian economics to change itself, and therefore funded Marx's analysis and writing for years. Only later did they write together *The Communist Manifesto.*[12]

Simultaneously, the dying days of the British Raj in India attempted to control occupied peoples in restricting access to food, raw materials, or naturally occurring salt. Note the challenge by Gandhi in leading the Indian "salt marches" nonviolently as but one expression of indigenous protest against the oppressive nature of such colonial economics. Gandhi's own adoption of wearing only *khadi*, the Indian homespun cloth, and his encouragement to his supporters to do the same, rejecting the reimportation of Western-style clothing, emphasized the importance of newly emerging nations to support their own economic practices.[13] Later historically, we see similar encouragements about economics, clothing, and land reform made by Ho Chi Minh in Vietnam as a way of rejecting French Indo-Chinese colonialism and the *laissez-faire* American-styled exploitative economic system imposed upon them.[14]

Following the crash of 1929, two things occurred. First, workers in the USA and associated nations were encouraged to believe that by absorbing a capitalist system in which "wealth was the driving factor" everyone would become "better off." Second, Britain and Scandinavian countries dropped out of the gold (exchange) standard, thus unhitching their economic fortunes from automatic linkage with the dollar's fluctuations.

J. K. Galbraith (1908–2006) rose to prominence during the Second World War when the US government appointed him to lead their inflation-combatting Office of Price Administration. Its work may have antagonized many, but it allowed Galbraith to test economic theory, begin a prolific writing career, and create an international platform (particularly during

11. Engels and McLellan, *Condition of the Working Class in England.*

12. Marx and Engels, *Communist Manifesto.*

13. Gandhi, *Story of My Experiments with Truth,* 407–9.

14. Duiker, *Ho Chi Minh,* 475–88.

President Kennedy's era) for him to advocate a "post-Keynesian economy." In his 1952 book, *American Capitalism: The Concept of Countervailing Power*,[15] Galbraith noted that the US economy was totally (and probably best) managed by the combination of big business, a strong labor market, and an activist government. He saw their interplay as countervailing power—in marked contrast to the virtual *laissez-faire* 1920s and 1930s. Galbraith wanted to call his 1958 book *Why the Poor are Poor* but was dissuaded by his wife and his publishers, and it came out as *The Affluent Society*.[16] It revealed Galbraith's central argument that a capitalist economy, such as the USA's, had to create a demand for products (however useful or not), engendering continual acquisition through advertising, despite Galbraith being personally critical of that. He argued that taxation must be used to enable the social infrastructure (e.g., education, road networks, "safety net provision") of the nation to grow apace. Galbraith was interventionist and described as a "post-materialist."

The Second World War had left a huge agenda. The Communist revolution in China isolated the then second-largest nation from the rest of the world. Its Maoist (rather than Marxist) economics saw its people ruled by a pampered, self-perpetuating oligarchy, which brutally suppressed the people, using food supply, fear, and mass starvation to control them.[17] Stalinist hardening of attitudes in the Soviet bloc led to the Cold War. The world was actively witnessing the rise of both Communism and individually powerful nations, with alternative economic models that did not retain simply peasant economies. The 1948 partitioning and independence of India heralded the end of the old colonialism and the beginning of a new economic world order.

The free world had its own problems; European nations had bankrupted themselves in their war efforts. President Truman's US administration recognized the potential to take control again of the free world economic system, having no desire to restrain its own capacity to run large trade surpluses with as many other nations as possible. A new fixed exchange rate, known as the "Bretton Woods system," was instigated, linking afresh other currencies to a known dollar rate; thus again controlling international money supply. To enable this, two organizations were set up. One was the International Monetary Fund (IMF), which became the capitalist

---

15. Galbraith, *American Capitalism*.
16. Galbraith, *Affluent Society*.
17. Fenby, *Penguin History of Modern China*.

world's "fire brigade"—and still is—despite Bretton Woods' 1970s demise. The second was a US-European partnership to create what subsequently became the Organization for Economic Cooperation and Development. In the USA, all this created room for Galbraith's post-Keynesian economic models to be exported throughout the free world.

The Marshall (George, not Alfred's!) Plan set out to dollarize Europe. It underfinanced Britain's renewal, causing the UK to have little involvement in the future control of Middle Eastern oil reserves, progressively "developing" other European economies at the USA's speed and expedience, while rehabilitating (western) Germany and Japan in its own capitalist modeling. In Jesus' days, the denarius and Roman domination created a *Pax Romana*; by the 1950s the USA was using its dollar clout and global muscle to declare a *Pax Americana*.

In the second half of the twentieth century, Milton Friedman (1912–2006) was among those leading economists who argued that the central bank would always have difficulty in forecasting the nature of both national and international money supply, leading to vast fluctuations in regional economies. Friedman saw direct links between inflation and money supply, having been harshly critical of the "Bretton Woods system," the Federal Reserve system, and Keynesian policies, then later such policies' creation of homeland "welfare dependency." His many writings clarifying his economic theories, called "monetarist," and his libertarian overview of social policies (e.g., gay rights, no military conscription, and negative taxation) helped him win the 1976 Nobel prize for economics.

Perhaps surprisingly, it was the monetarist Alan Greenspan, later chair of the Federal Reserve, who enabled both Thatcher and Reagan to utilize Friedman's monetarist thinking to determine transatlantic *laissez-faire* economic policies for the 1980s. From his earliest days, following the 1987 stock market crash, Greenspan's lengthy Federal Reserve tenure saw him rightly criticized as a "loose monetarist," allowing currencies and systems to fail before offering to clear them up, only then using US liquidity with hindsight. Despite criticism, Greenspan was a smart cookie, becoming a chief adviser to Deutsche Bank after his Fed days, and in early 2007 rightly predicting a 2008 global recession, which would profoundly affect the USA.

This brief, historically subjective essay is now almost too close to the present sufficiently to analyze changing theory in this generation. We look at some of the main issues and problems in the next chapter. But there are new voices and expressions about how things *could* be done and economies managed. Like Friedman, Friedrich Hayek (1899–1992) was a penetrative analyst and Nobel laureate, who recognized that economic theory had to be advocated within a broader social and philosophical framework.

That broader approach is essential to this book's trajectory, finding support in the writings of E. F. Schumacher and the "Ecological Economics" school. As we discover in chapter 3, the well-argued commitment of Jeffrey Sachs, Joseph Stiglitz, and Herman Daly, all renowned World Bank economists, are also within it. However, in Europe, the writings of economists such as Molly Scott Cato and Thomas Piketty, alongside those of popular commentators (e.g., Naomi Klein), build upon Schumacher's beginnings, establishing an alternative, if not an eco-, economic school. In chapter 10, I offer conclusions about how important all these writers are in forcing economic theory to turn another corner.

Key economic practices

We can choose to advocate a society like the Wild West frontier or the Scottish Border Reivers' territory, when what you have and can keep, normally by force, allows you to be "king of the castle," creating your own wealth to provide literally everything you and your dependents need.

The world is not like that. In various configurations we live in society with each other, with varying levels of interdependence. In that mutual reliance, there have to be some rules (e.g., looting or taking by force is wrong), and once we step beyond subsistence agrarian societies, something will become currency, be it furs, slaves, food, salt, or gold. Economic principles and practices develop.

Until recent decades, the Westernized nations of North America, the UK, and Eurozone as well as Australasia have effectively acted together as a control and a brake on the global economy. They have had the ability to control both the growth of nations such as Japan, and also the restrictions upon the prices of products from the developing nations, such as those from Southeast Asia or Africa. They have done this by extending their own principles of taxation, by commodifying almost everything, yet inadvertently creating an uncontrollable global monetary system and not truly recognizing the power of "the new kids on the block."

Taxation

Was it not Benjamin Franklin who said, "In this world nothing can be said to be certain, except death and taxes"? The previous part of this chapter affirms how taxation is a necessary part of society. If we want roads (and road repairers), education for our children or a judicial system, these have to be paid for and some system of federal or city taxation is required to do so. The key principle is how such taxation should be applied: should it be progressively applied to income or to the amount of one's possessions? Should we have a "purchase tax" upon some (or all?) goods and services? All civilizations have had taxation of some sort. Remember, even Jesus had to ask his followers for a coin, bearing the mark of their Galilean oppressors, and tell them to pay their due taxes with "render to Caesar . . ." (Mark 12:17). We return to the question of "just taxation" in chapter 2.

"Commodification"

In his life-enhancing novel *The Alchemist* Paulo Coelho said, "Everything in life has its price," which is daily misquoted by nearly everyone. In today's labor markets, there is a salary to catch every worker whereas people-traffickers know that even their sisters and brothers have a market value! Whether it's a new fridge or the latest SUV, we understand that everything even natural resources have their ultimate price—whatever their scarcity. This is the frightening contemporary construct/practice which is known as "commodification." Part of Marx's helpful analysis was to remind us that society becomes a danger to itself when it commodifies labor, people or those goods which traditionally did (and even *should*) not have a price put upon them.

The "global monetocracy"

The mind-blowing 2003 book *Gaian Democracies* first coined and thus popularized the phrase "the global monetocracy," which has easily slipped into mass-media usage. The "global monetocracy" concept is the world-wide phenomenon that now money talked and commercially was acting transnationally. Just like General Motors, Coca-Cola, and—how many more would you like to name?

Later we shall return to why this book proved helpful in "redefining globalization and people power."[18] As the noughties evolved, so did the role of transnational companies. For many years, we had watched as the über-rich moved to tax havens, such as Monaco, Panama, or the Cayman Islands. Now companies began emulating individuals, moving their taxable bases to the jurisdiction where they could pay least tax. Nowhere was this more apparent to Europeans than with the global internet-based companies such as Amazon or Google, or those representing the city lifestyle, such as Starbucks or the international banks. Individuals and consumer groups increasingly questioned the injustice that such companies with huge incomes paid little or no tax in the territories generating that wealth.

In January 2016, the UK's former right-wing Chancellor of the Exchequer[19] advocated, in a much-publicized interview, that old-style / "Galbraithian" graduated "corporation tax" (levied on profits) should be scrapped in favour of taxation upon sales in the country concerned. "It is also grossly unfair on smaller businesses, who are unable to shift profits between tax jurisdictions and have to pay the full amount due under UK law . . . . While multinationals can artificially shift profits to whatever tax jurisdictions they choose, sales are where they are, and can't be shifted . . . the UK should take the lead in implementing this much-needed reform."[20] No wonder his comments were globally reported across those nations where the US$, £-sterling or euros are traded. Time for change.

Recognizing the new players

UK economics professor Jim O'Neill began inventing acronyms for the recently developing circles of countries as serious economic players. His first was BRIC, referring to Brazil, Russia, India, and China. Consider all the media furor about social and economic conditions surrounding the high spending for the 2016 Rio Olympics or the challenges created by Russia's GazProm in the Arctic (1) or the increasing economic influence of the world's one billion-plus nations of India and China. O'Neill's second acronymic circle, MINT, meaning Mexico, Indonesia, Nigeria, and Turkey, are just entering the global stage. O'Neill's circles of shared economic

18. Madron and Jopling, *Gaian Democracies.*

19. Lawson, *View from Number 1.*

20. Interview with Lord Nigel Lawson, in *The Daily Telegraph*, January 30, 2016.

development are now challenging the supremacy of former key players, such as the USA or Germany, in determining global economic policy.

The bottom line

Capitalist China's 2015/16 unilateral devaluation of its own currency, the *yuan*, was the clarion declaring a new global economic order. No longer did a major economy need to heed the USA and indeed it could significantly wound the dollar system. The old days of Venetian ducats, the gold standard, Bretton Woods, or the IMF having any real semblance of control of world economics is probably dying. "China's reforms are re-shaping the global economy and global politics. Soviet reforms beginning in the 1980s and changes in India in the early 1990s were no doubt inspired in part by China's successes."[21] No longer will the US dollar be able to ride over the world's hill, like the US Cavalry, to sort out the mess, as successively Keynes, Galbraith, Friedman, and Greenspan once believed. "In future years, the rising power of China and India could further wound US pride and self-confidence, and further ratchet-up global tensions."[22]

It is the transnational corporations and the mega-sized (both in population size and financial clout or growth) nations who now "rule the roost." As Keith Hebden, the director of the UK's Urban Theology Unit has prophetically written:

> So we reward genetically-modifying, patent-hungry monsters like Monsanto [a food production transnational], even though they create starvation, slavery and environmental disaster, because they dazzle us with the promise of technological and economic salvation. We shop till we drop because Marks and Spencer tell us that there is a lifestyle attached to the sweater we buy. We sacrifice the lives of our military because the oil- and gas-guzzling monsters— which isn't only the oil industry but all systems dependent upon fossil fuels—demand that we feed them ever more of the earth's natural resources. We are told that they live to serve us but deep down we all know that we live to serve them. The monsters are our masters.[23]

21. Sachs, *End of Poverty*, 169.

22. Sachs, *Commonwealth*, 8.

23. Hebden, *Seeking Justice*, 30–31.

In terms of the global *oikos*, the USA, UK, Eurozone, and Australasia no longer "call the shots." Many of the new players do not believe as we Westerners believe, nor value human lives as we do. Some have better worldviews about their natural resources or native animals and plants than Westernized nations do. The world that Western economists have created for us will not be the one which our grandchildren inherit—if we still have a planet by then. We have to look afresh at what happens when that (meaning "our") kind of economic system goes awry. Then what we can do is to start building a better world for those yet unborn—as well as ourselves.

2 Foolishness to the Greeks

There is a new generation of internationally respected economists who work across continents, writing intelligible patterns of alternative economic theory. What they share is an understanding of what *is* happening as the developing, corporately accepted theories of last century's economics do not seem to be working in our new economic world order.

Twentieth-century capitalism has created "the new monsters":

- I have a brave UK-born friend, who has retired with his Chinese wife to a provincial city in China. Many of our mutual acquaintances have voiced concerns for them because of the increasing inequalities that may re-erupt in the new Chinese capitalist economy. How long before that economy becomes the world's largest, overtaking the USA's, and is then deciding the "ground rules" for us all?[1]

- A few years ago, I heard one of the new generation economists, Yanis Varoufakis, speak in a London School of Economics public lecture. He spoke of the new global minotaur within economics. The minotaur is a mythical beast that devours all in its wake, ultimately bringing tragedy upon the nation that does not comply with its demands. I found Varoufakis, his thesis, and now his writings totally credible;[2] he is a Keynesian, believing in altruistic economics.

- Both my own and my friends' world travels beyond the civilized free world tell of inequality. The rich are getting richer, the poor are getting

1. Jacques, *When China Rules the World.*
2. Varoufakis, *Global Minotaur.*

poorer, and the planet still burns in its own carbon emissions as the "haves" seek to acquire more at the expense of the "have nots."

If you are uncertain, think about what is happening to the Nenet, those caribou herders in Arctic Yamal.

Crashes and the failure of corporate theory

Humanity naturally favors a capitalist system, because of greed. We have to work against our very human nature not to "acquire bigger barns" (Luke 12:18) and then fill them. I have many friends and acquaintances who believe in a "simplicity of living," in developing low-impact lifestyles; more of them in chapter 9. But the faith of those Quakers, Mennonites, and other radical Christians can seem like "foolishness to the Greeks" (1 Cor 1:22–25)—those who live in their orbits of self-centred philosophy, greed, and acquisition.

Even the Romans conquered Europe with a capitalist model. The old joke that their legions' standards, declaring SPQR, meant "Small Profits, Quick Returns," is of course false. But its true Latin meaning of *Senatus Populus Que Romanus* is "the Senate and People of Rome," and was attached to the coinage and documents of the Roman Empire; possession of either implied acceptance of the empire's dominion over one. In other words, every aspect of life and death was based on the empire's rules. That is also how monetary systems work—or not.

The South Sea Company formed in 1711 was a public-private company designed to consolidate and thus reduce national debts, which naturally occurred in the development of the British colonies, including the Americas. The company was given the trading monopoly for South America, attracted much inward investment without any realistic trading prospect or even transactions, then financially collapsed before 1720. The bubble had burst, huge losses by investors were sustained, and the phrase "South Sea Bubble" became subsequently applied to any form of dubious investment. As a result, the UK Bubble Act of 1720 forbade the creation of any similarly styled joint stock companies. Yet after the great Wall Street Crash of 1929, the phrase "South Sea Bubble" was applied to the trading euphoria that preceded it. This crash had involved much speculative investment, stock/commodity prices free-falling and heralding a decade-long financial depression for all the industrialized nations.

But did the Western world learn? The previous chapter about economic theory tells of the postwar crawl for the free world to become partners rather than slaves of US-led capitalist domination. It was not just Gordon Gekko who thought he was a god on Wall Street. The plain fact is there are too many more, thinking they could live without much regulation in their expansionist speculations. Either side of the Atlantic, the worker power of unions was crushed and statutorily emasculated. For nearly twenty years, the US promotion of almost unpayable subprime mortgages occurred, spiralling many families down into poverty and once-fine cities (e.g., Detroit) into decline. Traders operated from less-regulated market centers, with insufficient supervision, occasionally with calamitous result. Do you remember the collapse of Barings Bank—and why it happened?

In 2008, all three of Iceland's national, privately owned banks had huge commercial investments in UK and Dutch infrastructure projects. Then because of the international trading crisis they could not create the necessary short-term refinancing. Therefore the whole Icelandic domestic economy tumbled, forcing austerity upon its people, overseas financial losses, and the nationalization of one of those three banks. Bolstered by its growth through US dollar support, Japan's economy majorly stuttered as both the "Asian tiger" and Pacific Rim economies slowed by 2008.

The outworking of this was the Great Crash of 2008, regarded as worse than that of 1929, which precipitated a global liquidity crisis. Should governments devalue their currency and print more money? The consequent downturn in economic activity led to a five-year (2008–12) global recession, significant rises in commodity prices (including oil), overwhelmingly contributing to the European "sovereign debt" crisis. Multiple African and Asian nations reported that their previously growing economies had stalled or even entered decline. There were runs on several UK financial houses, including the one that bankrupted Northern Rock, as well as in the USA and Europe. Internationally renowned companies such as Lehmann Brothers went to the wall.

What must be recognized is that we live in an interwoven global economy as one household/*oikos*. No amount of US legislation, such as the 2010 Dodd-Frank Act (to protect consumers and investors) can reach beyond their national boundaries, nor protect America from the effects of another global recession. Given current economic practice, if the USA cannot protect itself, no other country can—as global recession is spectacularly devastating and one day will be irredeemable.

An even more crass development is the current US-European Union Transatlantic Trade and Investment Partnership, or TTIP, which is opposed by many Europeans, socialist groups, green, and other "people parties." Basically this will allow transnational conglomerates to sue governments/ nations for loss of trade if their national restrictions diminish those transnationals' profit margins or right to trade.

The question remains—how much has corporate theory got it wrong? And if so, is there a present alternative? What happens to defaulting countries now and how can we arrive at some consideration of an alternative future? That future is the subject of the next chapter, and the journey which answering these questions entails forms the balance of this one.

Did Kropotkin, Marx, & co. get it wrong?

The problem is not necessarily capitalism, in itself, but that voluntary socialism has failed the world and its nations. Commentators speculate as to whether it was this dilemma that caused Marx and Engels to write *The Communist Manifesto*.

Since my teenage years, I have been an avid reader of Kropotkin and Tolstoy. Kropotkin (1842–1921) was a polymath and philosopher who renounced his aristocratic background to align himself with the peasantry by conviction. The titles of his three major works—*The Conquest of Bread*,[3] *Fields, Factories and Workshops*,[4] and *Of Mutual Aid: A Factor of Evolution*[5] (all on my shelves since I was a teenager) tell of his desire for and advocacy of an egalitarian society, free from centralized government control and organized by local voluntary associations of workers and their families. He was critical of the 1917 Bolshevik Revolution's violence, having already warned in *The Conquest of Bread* that any such communistic state, predicated upon violence, had already sown the seeds of its downfall, including an almost logical return to capitalism. Subsequent events in the USSR and China have proved him to be correct in this.

Tolstoy (1828–1910) also renounced his aristocratic background, undergoing a profound Christian conversion in the 1870s to become a fervent anarchist, pacifist, and coworker with his former estate servants (much to the chagrin of his domineering wife). His pacifism influenced Gandhi

3. Kropotkin, *Conquest of Bread*.

4. Kropotkin, *Fields, Factories and Workshops*.

5. Kropotkin, *Mutual Aid*.

and Martin Luther King Jr., just as his writings have alerted millions to the plight of the common man or woman when forced to live within the hierarchy and economic system of prevailing Russian society.

It is clear that Marx knew the thought and writings of Kropotkin and Tolstoy (as well as similarly minded others) and, as the notes for his economic work reveal,[6] was profoundly affected by the inability of ordinary people to have control of their economic and social destiny. Obviously that sits in diametric opposition to those who believe in self-seeking and capitalist hierarchical societies. But, to the radical Christian, Marx's economic reflections are clearly on the same page as the egalitarian "reign of God" teaching of Jesus of Nazareth, revealed in the Christian Gospels.

It becomes more than a Greek tragedy when the contest between common humanity and the ruling economic system becomes overwhelming—as our next section reveals.

Agony[7]

The creation of a common currency—the euro—across the majority of nations of the European Union in 1999 was fraught with many potential and ongoing problems. The participating countries became known as the Eurozone and, without formal political and federal union (such as in the USA or former USSR), relied on each participant nation's government acting within the defined rules and economic treaties. The latter tied all those nations together with demanded monetary policies, requiring all—whether at the top or bottom of the financial "elastic"—to behave and act similarly. Before joining the Eurozone, EU member countries must spend two years within the European Exchange Rate Mechanism, to help create this compliance.

The EU required its constituent national governments to be strong enough to put their "own house in order." No longer could individual nations simply decide to lower taxes or increase pension levels without ensuring they could "balance their own books" and not exceed agreed borrowing levels. I was living in France when this really began to bite and noted how the French government had to resist the calls for a statutory "working week" of fewer hours, or for lowering the pensionable age for state workers, or raising pensions but not taxes. This took cross-party strength and philosophical resolve. Other countries such as Ireland, Portugal, and Spain

---

6. Marx, *Grundrisse*.

7. From *agon*, which is the classical Greek word for "contest."

found their economies faltering, requiring strong fiscal remedies upon their own peoples, in order to meet the demands of the European Central Bank and their partner nations within the Eurozone. The fear of domino economic downfall brought forward the word *contagion* in our economic vocabularies. The nation that fell hardest was Greece.

Following the ending of the Greek military junta in 1974, many restrictions were lifted—including letting long-haired backpackers (like me) travel relatively freely and bring in the so-called tourist dollar, which was traded for a sackful of drachmas. But Greek government policies were at best somewhat erratic. The über-rich could choose whether to join in or how much state taxation they would pay. There was political expedience and laxity in policy, increasing pensions, guarantees of state employment, etc. Some tell me there were allegations of political corruption . . . while those same politicians had to comply with the conditions for becoming part of the Eurozone. Many of the island or rural poor lived in subsistence poverty, hardly earning enough to pay any tax. In any household (Greek: *oikos*) or nation, the bills have to be paid and Greece's were not.

I found I was a natural supporter of PASOK, the PanHellenic Socialist Movement, using my visits and increasing Greek fluency to chat with islanders, ferrymen, and small farmers about why this social democratic movement commanded so much popular support. One major reason was that Greeks are proud of the civic understanding of being a *polis*—a democratic people with a 2,500-year history. Even the illiterate had a stronger understanding of "the people's decision" than I encountered in Britain, northern Europe, or North America. PASOK only lost their political dominance when the Eurozone's imposed austerity measures hit the Greek populace in the successive 2010 and 2012 bailouts. It was little surprise to me when the harder-left *Syriza* coalition was elected in January 2015 on an even tougher anti-austerity platform. An inevitable collision was set up—as Greece defaulted again on its international loans (against its background of political inabilities to comply with financial needs/policies)—between *Syriza*'s own hard-line stance and the European Central Bank's demands for immediate compliance, which would mean accepting further austerity.

Whatever the rights and wrongs of the understandable decision of the Greek Referendum in July 2015 to reject the imposition of further austerity measures, one casualty was Yanis Varoufakis, the internationally respected economist and then Greek Finance Minister. He resigned the morning after the referendum's results was known, saying that Greek Prime Minister

Tsipras had agreed with him that other Eurozone finance ministers would find it easier to try finding a different "bailout package" for the Greeks without Varoufakis in the room. Across Europe, media reports stated that Varoufakis tweeted to his international followers: "I shall wear the creditors' loathing with pride."

To many outside Europe, it was hard to immediately understand the reasons why the Greeks should reject the bailout package offered by the Eurozone countries. However, tracking both societal and financial restrictions during the period from the 2010 crisis through the 2012 bailout to 2015 reveals many human reasons for this. In that five-year period:

- Many salaries had been gradually halved to a level of €600/US$675/£450 per calendar month.

- Nearly 60 percent of all pensioner families' incomes had become less than €500/US$560/£375 per calendar month.

- Over 50 percent of workers aged under twenty-five were unemployed. For workers aged over twenty-five, that figure was approximately 25 to 30 percent, depending upon location (e.g., city, tourist resort, island). Many city and government workers went to their offices daily, simply to retain their jobs despite not being paid.

- The provision of universal healthcare had undergone a 25 percent cut in both provision and delivery.

For many of those already living in isolated—mountain, rural, or island—poverty as well as the middle classes, who were possibly supporting their adult, college-educated children on a single, halved salary, further austerity could not be contemplated. They had to vote "*Oxi*"—"No"—and reject the Eurozone's further bailout because of the increasing austerity measures and higher taxation demanded.

Greece was the first modernized postwar country to default on its loan from the World Bank. This put the Greeks in the same dubious defaulter's "bucket" as the Taliban's Afghanistan or Mugabe's Zimbabwe. Summer 2015 wore tortuously onward, as the Tsipras government was humiliatingly forced to accept an IMG and ECB package that was even more austere than that rejected by the July 2015 referendum. France tried to help Greece draft domestic measures to receive that bailout. Nations such as Finland became increasingly hawkish as did the penitent but previously failing Portugal. Finally, by autumn 2015, that Eurozone bailout had been agreed on, but at what cost to *Syriza*, and the poorest of the Greek taxpayers and pensioners, as well as national pride in the meaning of democracy?

Even so, summer 2016 saw that bailout demanding the increase of VAT (purchase tax) from 16 to 25 percent on all goods and services, inflicting further damage upon Greek tourist income, precipitating further hardship.

Was it not Aristophanes who had his Athenian hero, Dikaiopolis, say of the conflict with the Spartans: "Greeks will never be free until we sack the clowns who rule us"?[8] As the condition of Spartan austerity hurts more Greeks, there is much more to come as increasingly that proud people questions what it means to be ruled from afar. As Joseph Stiglitz, the World Bank's chief economist, maintained: "Europe's austerity measures are a suicide pact."

Taxation

A major part of Greece's recent problems has been the (political) inability to create and sustain a progressive but uniform taxation across all its people. The lesson for us is in the key question: what kind of society and state intervention do we want?

Religious/church taxes

The Bible is full of encouragement to bring of our best before God. At harvest time we are to "put the first fruits in a basket and go to the altar" (Deut 26:1–10). Yet we are also enjoined by Jesus that if we are at enmity with a sister or brother, we should leave the basket and go and seek reconciliation first. The Hebrew practices of offering animal sacrifices are still part of what we often call "pagan cultures." It is unsurprising that human nature seeks to get away with the minimum and so there was almost a temple tariff of what needed to be sacrificed to expiate for one's individual sin. It was graduated or progressive: the poor man might need to sacrifice only two doves while the rich man might need to offer a goat.

Alongside this, the biblical practice of "tithing" occurred. This means giving the first 10 percent of one's income or harvest to God or his earthly representative! My friend, Stuart Murray, has written a penetrating analysis

8. Aristophanes, "Acharnians."

of this practice, in *Beyond Tithing*, arguing that although tithing may be biblical, it is not Christian. The promotion of tithing by evangelical Christians must be interrogated, not just on those grounds, but also because it creates a minimalist attitude to Christian generosity. It allows tithers to say "job done" easily—particularly if US tax breaks are involved. This is in marked contrast to the generous lifestyles of my politically radical friends, family, Anabaptist and Mennonite *compañeros*.

Before the Industrial Revolution, every English parish had its tithe barn so the priest could oversee and collect the due tithes from every parishioner. In Lutheran countries, the tithe was converted into a tax and collected by the state authorities, who passed it on to the church. Gradually Lutheranism has moved from an "opt-out" to an "opt-in" church tax policy, across Germany and Scandinavia, massively reducing denominational income and its stewardship theology built upon tithing.

Learning from "secular" Europe

Late nineteenth-century Germany provided a model of "state socialism," which found echoes in US "progressivism" and the UK's "social liberalism." Chancellor Bismarck's policies then have evolved into present-day Germany's welfare state. Benefits apply equally to all German citizens but it is an individual's contribution and positive taxation history that determines what they receive. Similarly in France, French nationals (or more precisely their employers) pay highly to provide social benefits and high-quality health care to workers and their families, both during employment and in retirement. However the French have "top-up" payments for everything, including doctors' appointments, health tests, and medication; the French poor can reclaim some or all of those payments through a convoluted bureaucratic process. In other words, benefits are "means-tested" for all citizens but refugees, incomers, etc. in both France and Germany receive fewer automatic benefits.

This is unlike Britain, where the post-1945 Beveridge Report created a nationwide system of non-means-tested benefits, including the National Health Service. That was fine when most health care was palliative, surgery was risky, and life expectancy lower. In today's UK, the country cannot afford universal health care without making difficult choices:

- What treatments should be freely available to all? E.g., should infertility treatment or cancer care or diabetes clinics take priority? What happens when different regions (therefore zip codes) have different answers?

- Should there be automatic "means-testing" (anathema to UK socialists) of all benefits? The British already pay for much dental and optical care and prescriptions in England.

Those who favor a universal "Obamacare" health provision need to recognize these arguments, as well as the growing US problems associated with diabetes and advancing medical science, when making their long-term policy decisions.

To return to the key question: what kind of society and state intervention do we want? Crudely, the choice lies between a "high taxation-high welfare-free education" society or a "low taxation-low welfare-basic education" package. Scandinavia and the Netherlands favor the former. In Sweden, taxation is progressive, rising quickly to 50 percent. For a single person, with subsidized housing, this level bites at a US$45,000/UK£32,000 salary level. Little is means-tested, except housing subsidy and city taxes. Philosophically, the USA, Canada, Australasia, and Germany have few problems with means-testing, whereas Britain and Scandinavia do.

How we encourage (and vote for) society's organization not only determines its financing and social polity but often also our thinking about how we share both monetary and community wealth with others than our historic citizens.

Both US Republicans and UK Conservatives would disagree with me but, for the record, I am a "high taxation-high welfare-free education" advocate. But I am also a vocal supporter of the debate that says that *every* country should have both a minimum and a maximum wage, incurring 95 percent taxation beyond the top hourly level. Elsewhere, I have already detailed my much lower income needs[9] but essentially I believe in simplifying our lifestyle and needs sufficiently to thrive on the state-recognized living (minimum) wage while using any surplus for charitable and other *pro bono* work.

Finally, I want to commend the Irish system that enables artists, musicians, sports stars, actors, etc., who are relatively temporary high earners, to spread their income over several years, paying the appropriate level of

---

9. Francis, *Shalom*, 154.

tax in each of those years. With a maximum number of applicable years, dependent upon career length, this seems equitable to both the individual and the wider society.

What would Jesus do?

Jesus shared our human nature and well understood the innate desire to get something for nothing that afflicts us all. Indeed, he reminded his closest followers to "render unto Caesar . . ." (i.e., pay the due taxes), he confronted the corrupt tax collector Zacchaeus, inspiring the latter's reparation, and taught many parables about the value of money. Jesus taught that money, resources, and food are to be shared *if* God's intentions are to be fulfilled—and those who follow his words and ways now must share that same intention.

Therefore, I believe that the Western world must increase taxation to provide both overseas aid and interest-free development loans. Failure will bring the alternative that rich nations get richer and the poor countries poorer. The current European migrant crisis is symptomatic of that. Tragically, the guys in my local bar who complain about such migration are not always the first or worst to avoid paying tax. Rich people pay accountants to do that for them.

Serving God and Mammon

Jesus was very clear in declaring the dilemma between the intentions of God's reign and serving one's self-interest in pursuit of money: "You cannot serve God and money" (Matt 6:24). Unequivocal! Jesus declared God and money to be two distinct masters, between whom choice has to be made. For the disciple of Jesus, there is no choice but to accept God's intention, as revealed in the words and ways of Jesus.

For too long, there have been many rich men (and women) metaphorically stuffing camels through the eye of needles to try to prove otherwise (Matt 19:24). But "Go sell all that you have and give it to the poor" (Luke 18:22), "If anyone has two coats, let him give one to the man without a coat" (Luke 3:11), and the Parable of the Rich Man's Feast (Luke 14:12–24) are also unequivocal. When I open my closet full of shirts and suits, I know that Jesus' direct word is just as much for me as for the richest people in the world—and you as well.

Jesus' own ministry, and that of Peter, Paul, and the other apostles as well as the ongoing early church has always relied upon the unstinting generosity and hospitality of its materially blessed supporters. There is nothing wrong with making money but we must do it in both ethical and Earth-friendly ways. Then it is what we do with it and how we share our material resources that will demonstrate our commitment to the "reign of God," as revealed in Jesus of Nazareth.

Just as voluntary socialism and brutally enforced Communism have failed as alternatives, the endless pursuit of capitalism is being questioned by both our finite environmental/ecological limitations and an exponentially growing global population. How we live with those constraints demands some prophetic alternatives. The next chapter seeks to offer some initial pointers, thinking, and questions.

3 Come on Over and Help Us

This chapter's title is my paraphrase of Paul the missionary-evangelist's vision of a Macedonian (a northern Greek) plea to come and help them understand the words and ways of Jesus. Critique is all very well but well-researched Christians need to be able to respond helpfully in advocating creative, Earth-friendly, economic alternatives—rooted in the words and ways of Jesus.

Costanza summarized the status quo: "Modern economics typically continues to assume that society is simply the sum of its individuals, the social good is the sum of individual wants, and markets automatically guide individual behaviour to the common good."[1] As the previous two chapters reveal, this is not true. However well and good economic theory has evolved (cf. chapter 1), if it is no longer "fit for purpose" (a legal standard) because of its inherent systems, such as the Eurozone, or if "wealth inequalities" are damaging the poorest of the poor—and others (cf. chapter 2), then change is needed. If we are believers and followers of the words and ways of Jesus, in declaring the "reign of God," such change is vital, life-giving, and demanded. Now!

Economics as if people mattered

In 1973, a friend gave me a copy of E. F. Schumacher's *Small is Beautiful*[2] and it illuminated my world and questioning faith with a searchlight's bril-

1. Costanza, ed., *Introduction to Ecological Economics*, 24.
2. Schumacher, *Small is Beautiful*.

liance. Its subtitle—*A Study of Economics as if People Mattered*—has slipped into the parlance of thinking people.

Schumacher (1911–77) was a German internee, who fell under Keynes's influence and patronage, becoming for two decades the Chief Economic Adviser to the UK's National Coal Board. That coal industry was central to Britain's postwar industrial and economic growth. He went to Burma as an economic consultant, learning well in reciprocation. There, he coined a phrase, of which various versions have also moved into common parlance: "Production from local resources for local needs by local people is the most rational way of economic life." Schumacher termed this as "Buddhist economics" and used it as the central part of his advocacy to many other developing world nations, which invited his help.

"The keynote of Buddhist economics is simplicity and non-violence,"[3] affirming the purity of the community in which each individual's labor brings forth food and utilitarian products for the good of all. I believe the earthly Jesus would be encouraging that, too. Schumacher wrote widely, although *Small is Beautiful* remains his seminal work. His 1997 text, *A Guide for the Perplexed*, rejects the atheism of his youth and criticizes the "materialistic scientism" of his life's work, revealing his fascination with Buddhism and mysticism, finally (and incidentally) his 1971 conversion to Catholicism.

Another doubting Thomas

My postman complained as I tore open another book parcel, this time one containing Thomas Piketty's *Capital in the Twenty First Century*,[4] that a 700-page hardback would never fit in my mailbox. Piketty is a brilliant, globally recognized French economist, whose work majors upon wealth and income inequality. His *Capital* reviews the past 250 years with its attendant wealth distribution and unequal concentrations. It points towards the emerging facts that, in Westernized/developed nations, capital returns outstrip rates of economic growth, thus increasing future wealth inequalities. This Thomas (Piketty) doubts that traditional economic theory and practice can cure, or even alleviate this; therefore root-and-branch economic change is needed. Piketty's solution is for capital redistribution based upon progressive taxation on all global wealth: land, resources, and finance.

3. Ibid., 47.
4. Piketty, *Capital in the Twenty First Century*.

Ecological economics

Thanks to the liberation and ecofeminist theologians, Joerg Rieger[5] and Sallie McFague[6] respectively, I discovered the work of Robert Costanza[7] and "ecological economics." I further encountered the phrase through various writings of Herman Daly,[8] Jeffrey Sachs,[9] and Joseph Stiglitz,[10] all highly regarded World Bank economists as well as advisers to international NGOs and US presidents. We shall return to their writings later in this book.

Like Piketty, they all pose questions about the nature of economic growth, arguing that it cannot be done in a purist way, within a vacuum, assuming ongoing growth for all. It must take account of the world, the global ecology, and resources usage, which must limit the behavior/lifestyle of all people.

In its turn, this raises questions about truly costing everything. A car or closet or coffee does not just have a monetary cost but a planetary cost in each unit's production; the latter is often forgotten or not factored in. This is at the heart of ecological economics. Akin to neo-Marxian methodology, the cost of production is more than what is invoiced for constituent parts and labor. The true cost of production must be factored in too, whether there is one less tree or the process has used (too many) gallons of irreplaceable fossil fuel or that a production worker might have been progressively exposed to industrial illness (creating future health care costs) and so on.

Ecological economics challenges twentieth-century economic theory development. In the "Ecology" section that follows, we shall address how this must affect our decision-making about energy usage or whether we should retain fossil fuel reserves or exhaust them. The real cost is far greater than a monetary one and requires us to rethink our strategies for creating new wealth for communities and the potential for reinvestment, including in alternative sources of energy. This also requires good ecological science, strength of governance, and not being bullied by the transnationals. Let me offer an example which is growing in international credence.

5. Rieger, ed., *Liberating the Future.*
6. McFague, *Life Abundant.*
7. Costanza, ed., *Introduction to Ecological Economics.*
8. Daly, *Beyond Growth.*
9. Sachs, *Commonwealth.*
10. Stiglitz, *Making Globalisation Work*; Stiglitz, *Price of Inequality.*

The Shetland "model"[11]

The Shetland Islands lie 110 miles to the north of Scotland's mainland. This mainly treeless archipelago of fifteen inhabited islands forms part of a north-south chain of geological outcrops that divide the European North Sea from the Atlantic Ocean. The islands' capital, Lerwick, is further north than Stockholm (Sweden) or Oslo (Norway), which are both closer to London, England's capital, than is Lerwick itself.

It is not just the stark beauty of "the Shetlands" which have created its proportionately significant financial wealth but the bounty of North Sea oil and a strong Shetland financial policy. The Shetland Islands Council has benefited from strong independent thinking, helped by clear-minded and purposeful councillors, wise advice, and their distance from their meddling parent Westminster government in London.

The discovery of huge reserves of oil and gas under the North Sea meant that someone or their shareholders could benefit greatly. Commercial interests quickly recognized that the Shetland Islands were the prime northern location for "landing" these mineral reserves. The Islands' council acted prophetically in *only* allowing one giant terminal at Sullom Voe to be built, through which all oil and gas had to be routed. By 1978, these reserves were being tapped by millions of barrels (the international unit) rather than the bucketloads predicted by the doom merchants.

The key was that the Sullom Voe development could only go ahead if each company paid a royalty or tax upon each barrel landed. This was a financial masterstroke to which the multinational energy companies could do nothing but acquiesce and pay up. This created a wealth or bounty for each Shetlander of at least £9,500 by 2011.

But the further masterstroke was not to disperse that income individually but to use it collectively.[12] The initial £81m received has grown by "canny investment" (as the Scots put it), to its £227m in 2014—and it continues to grow. The capital received is never spent but instead is placed in the hands of the Shetland Charitable Trust which invests 80 percent of that capital in the international investment market, e.g. bonds, "renewables,"

11. Much of the information in this section was also broadcast (and available then globally via podcast) by the BBC on July 7, 2014, in a program entitled *Scotland: For Richer or Poorer?*

12. This is in marked contrast and philosophical opposition to the Alaskan scheme in which that state's oil wealth provides an annual Permanent Fund Dividend to each Alaskan resident who has more than twelve months' residency.

etc. The other 20 percent is invested locally or in Shetland-serving schemes, such as transport, infrastructure, education, or employment projects. If ever there can be beauty in a financial vehicle, it is this: that only a proportion of the investment income is invested thereby adding to the capital pot, helping create a rising future income.

Such investment has daily enhanced the lives of the majority of Shetlanders if not all indirectly. Already eight new leisure centers, some with international sports-standard pools have been built (on different islands). Care homes have also received generous funding, creating additional and better provision for the elderly. Also a museum and multipurpose arts center have been built and funding was provided to develop the annual, internationally renowned Shetland Folk (music) Festival—all further attracting the tourist dollar and euro.

As importantly for Shetland families, this inward investment has created jobs. Shetland's unemployment rates and figures in 2014 were less than half those of the UK mean average. This meant that these were less than a third of comparable figures on the Scottish mainland. This is why Shetland became such a hot topic for discussion and a player in the political rhetoric surrounding the September 2014 vote concerning Scottish independence from the United Kingdom.

Before the naysayers condemn this model or imply that it cannot work as it was based on a region of unspoilt islands with a low population (under 24,000 in 2011), the so-called "Shetland model" is attracting global attention. This economic model was used as a case study by the Norwegian government in the 1980s *before* all the effects that we can witness now could be assessed. Its efficiency and efficacy were prophetically visible then to the Scandinavian planners and politicians. Thus Norway set up a similar, economically beneficial, trust model in the 1990s to deal with the bounty of its own mineral wealth and hydroelectric resources. In turn, this created sufficient capital that Norway's fund is a key investor of at least 0.5 percent up to 2 percent of virtually every listed company across western Europe. Norway's figures can seem mind-blowing for the general reader as in approximately the first twenty years up to 2014, its fund has created £500b in capital wealth.

What this demonstrates is that despite the use of finite resources, either fossil fuel or mineral, long-term and growing capital wealth has been created. Politicians won both philosophical and economic arguments to retain that for the cooperative benefit of their respective peoples. Some minor but significant investment is in companies researching possibilities, practical alternatives, and replacement options when those finite resources are exhausted.

> Since "economics is the study of how scarce resources are allocated among competing ones"[13] a worldview of planetary living is necessarily economic . . . . For the universal household called Earth to survive and flourish, certain "house rules" must be obeyed. These "house rules" are ecological, economic ones, having to do with the just division of basic resources, among all the members of the family of life.[14]

The Shetland and consequent Norwegian models demonstrating such cooperative, economic probity and prophetic planning have huge current implications for every nation.

Challenging the system

The Nobel laureate Daniel Kahnemann has advocated that at least US$70,000 annually is *required* to ensure the average US citizen has enough disposable income to be happy. I know many US pensioners, Mennonites, and "downshifters" who are more than happy with much lower incomes. However, in Seattle, the home of Amazon, Microsoft, and Starbucks, a long-haired entrepreneur, who cofounded Gravity Payments (a credit card company) independently realized that his workers needed a US$70,000 annual salary to live even modestly in that city. That man, Dan Price, treated his company like a commune, cutting his own salary from US$1m to the same US$70,000 as his coworkers, funding their rise from his own pay cut. While admiring Price's idealism, I recognize that he must have turned the local labor market on its head, as everyone in Seattle now wants that salary level and other city employers got mad with him for it. How we challenge and even change the system requires careful management.

How Kropotkin, Marx, and Jesus got it right

I recall sitting in a French village bar with my then neighbours, discussing Kropotkin, and their insistence that his model of "community thought"

13. Hackett, *Environmental and Natural Resources Economics*, 4.
14. McFague, *Life Abundant*, 72.

was drawn straight from the French Revolution, which instituted "the commune" as the most local form of democratic collective.[15] In French communes, residents have a formal responsibility to ensure they share resources, including food, with their neighbors, helping out at seedtime, harvest, and times of illness, working together to ensure their common survival as a people. This was not about money, nor all having the same salary but sharing a common life as villagers. Pure Kropotkin—as he renounced his title to join the peasantry, to share in the common struggle.

What people believe they have helps them understand their sense of identity. In Roman times, those with seemingly little property except their own children were known as the *proletarii* from which we gain the English word *proletariat*. This term was helpfully appropriated by Karl Marx to describe those who are simply of the wage-earning class, almost at the bottom of society, not owning property nor the means of production. Popularly, the "lumpen proletariat" are those outcast, unemployed, and poorest at the very base of society. Marx envisaged that the mass proletariat should democratically own the means of production and saw that as the political goal of a truly egalitarian society, in which all could benefit and thrive. Without that, hierarchy and profit would suppress the worker, while the rich enjoyed the inequality of increasing wealth: back to Piketty and "ecological economics."

After Jesus' execution by the Romans, it is hardly surprising that his nearest followers went back to their familiar compass points of Galilee and fishing. There in the low sunlight of a new day, they were struggling to catch anything to feed the mouths that relied upon them. Then a seeming stranger called from the shore that they were to cast their nets in a different direction; they caught almost more than they could cope with (John 21:10–20). We need to listen to that same person, Jesus, however strange he may seem in the light of the new day, calling us to cast our nets and thinking in a different direction. After all, Jesus is the one who teaches that there will be "bread for all" if only we choose to share in the "reign of God" about how we live and use our resources together for the common good.

The Christian New Testament and the teaching of Jesus have more to say in developing new economic structures than has been previously accepted. Jesus becomes a necessary compass point. "In the countries of the overdeveloped Western world, it is frequently bondage to material possessions that prevents us from wholeheartedly following Jesus on the road."[16]

15. Kropotkin, *Conquest of Bread*.

16. Gill, *Life on the Road*, 90.

By the early 1980s, seminal European Green politics accepted: "Ir-respective of who owns the means of production, the unrelenting pursuit of growth and industrial expansion must necessarily degrade the planet and impoverish its people."[17] What was needed was a new way of economics that placed the needs of both the *whole* global community and the planet itself in the right balance.

"Community economics"

It was reading the New Testament, and learning about Jesus' peacemaking and "alternative economics" that transformed the life and thinking of Gandhi. In its turn that transformed British colonialism, and set forward the life of newly independent nations which have since become world players. Who might have believed in 1948 that a diminutive Indian, in homespun *khadi*, who advocated living communally and with Jesus-style simplicity, would change our world? But then people ask the same questions about the changes wrought by other followers of that itinerant Galilean teacher, called Jesus of Nazareth . . .[18]

The Scottish theologian and human ecologist Alastair McIntosh tells of his 1970s Hebridean upbringing, without mod-cons like refrigerators, when as a young man he caught too many fish on his line. So as he cycled back home, he stopped at each croft, offering them fresh fish for no payment as he did not want to see his already-caught surplus wasted. Some crofters gave him eggs or potatoes for his family.[19] The islanders lived with an alternative economic of "community sharing"—which still goes on today.

In the six Asian countries through which the mighty Mekong flows there is a behavioral pattern across several of the ethnic tribes. There, if someone's vegetable plot lies fallow, because of age, infirmity, or even sloth, other villagers come and plant up and work that land so that the homesteader does not starve. An altruistic (non-Christian but sometimes animist) philosophy provides that motivation—not money nor self-interest.

17. Porritt, *Seeing Green*, 48.

18. Francis, *Shalom*.

19. McIntosh, *Soil and Soul*, 28.

Cooperative thinking

Although there is some prehistory, it was in 1844 in northern England that the Rochdale Pioneers founded the first cooperative society equitably to sell food and flour to their members. "A co-operative is a participative business, not solely as a means of increasing its productivity, but because its legal structure compels participation. It is holistic."[20] From those humble beginnings grew a large cooperative movement in Britain and into Europe, with shops or supermarkets, pharmacies, farms, and funeral care. It is commonly assumed that the Soviet collective farms, whether as *sovkhozes* or *kholkozes* (two distinctly different patterns of regionally organized collectivism for agricultural production) drew their inspiration from this model.

Now, collectives/cooperatives are a growing business model across Europe, where all the workers (production and administrative) own the means of production and share any profits equally. In the UK, the supermarket chain Waitrose, and its parent cooperative, the John Lewis Group, ably demonstrate this pattern of community economics. Perversely, despite their quality goods and idealistic collectivism, both Waitrose and other John Lewis group stores are known for their upmarket pricing and range, which are less affordable for the poor.

The traditional, hierarchical, profit-driven business system can be challenged. Some of my favorite cookbooks are drawn from the Moosewood Restaurant in Ithaca, New York, where eighteen folks collectively run this internationally known, predominantly vegetarian restaurant, by each taking turns from cooking, through waiting on tables, to washing up, while all sharing in the menu-planning and book-writing. Cooperatives, in their different styles and sizes, are a viable commercial model, which demonstrates that "economics as if people matter" is a strong enough principle to reorder society for the benefit of all.

In their own way, that is exactly what the Shetland Islands Council has done. Their model has stood a "test of time" and one of transition to Norway. Perhaps the reason that it is not yet universally acknowledged is that many Westernized nations want more than their fair share, which means more than enough to live as God intends for his people and this planet.

20. Sawtell, "Co-operatives," 55.

Lagom is enough

There is a wonderful Swedish word and concept, *lagom*, which permeates their whole society. Literally it means "team around" but practically, everyone understands it to say "not too little, not too much." When food is passed around the family meal table or at a community picnic or congregational potluck supper, everyone exercises *lagom* so everyone is fed. As a nation, Sweden's high taxation enables *lagom* so everyone receives the highest quality medical or social care, and so on. *Lagom* is a philosophy and theology of "enough."

In the mid-1970s, UK churches were challenged theologically and economically via a slim book, *Enough is Enough*,[21] by Bishop John Taylor, questioning our acquisitional (if not greedy) and money-centered lifestyle. Much more recently, Dietz and O'Neill wrote an excellent book, *Enough is Enough: Building a Sustainable Economy in a World of Finite Resources*;[22] the title explains its thesis and trajectory. It is a call to reject "growth upon economic growth" in favor of simply enough—but from a non-theological perspective. In this book I go a step further in calling for the global community's dimension to be similarly challenged within a theology of "enough." Remember that *lagom* requires a whole society in every local community to share this understanding if "enough" is to prevail.

Health care and social justice

From the days of Thomas Malthus and the writings of Paul Ehrlich, there have been arguments fairly positing the view that at some future point Earth's population will become unsustainable.[23] The comparison between the USA and the UK, with their respective insurance- and taxation-based provisions of medical and social care, are illustrative.[24] We know that in 2016 in the UK over 30 percent of adults were classed as "obese," whereas in the USA the figure is approaching a staggering 65 percent. This has huge implications not only for weight-related conditions, from diabetes through heart disease to skeletal problems (e.g. hip replacements), but also how

21. Taylor, *Enough is Enough*.

22. Dietz and O'Neill, *Enough is Enough*.

23. Francis, *What in God's Name*, 26–28.

24. Obtaining accurate and comparable figures for all this book's markets proved impossible.

society will pay for, even afford, the high costs of the care needs created. Add into this the fact that by 2030, two million people aged over sixty-five of the UK's projected population of seventy million will be childless. US actuarial figures suggest a higher percentage in this respect. This means that individuals with health needs will either have to pay a lot more towards their own costs or society will need to accept a greater mutual financial responsibility because otherwise the alternative of the elderly and/or sick dying on the streets will become a nightmare scenario.

Everybody recognizes that Westernized standards of health care, as in Australasia, Europe, the UK, and the USA, can never be afforded ecologically or economically across South America, Asia, and Africa. The simple costs of maintaining a heli-ambulance (even if they could land!) emergency service is mind-bogglingly beyond the economics of nearly every developing world nation: just consider the logistics. Location does affect projected human longevity. But the right to better health care is part of the advocacy of the World Health Organization and Westernized nations have to be prepared to fund that more fully, fairly, and consistently. A simple solution would be a US25c/UK15p levy on every pack of Westernized nation medication to be given directly to the WHO for funding better local initiatives in the less developed world.

And so?

We return to the global human implications of such health care issues in chapter 8, when we also look at the role of housing cooperatives, local exchange trading systems, and credit unions as strategic tools in changing and challenging economic expectations.

"See Venice and die . . ."

My marriage had been in trouble for a long time—was I just too busy as a pastor? We chose a Venice vacation as a *Don't Look Now*-style[25] rediscovery of what we once had. While there, my obvious arrhythmia and severe breathlessness indicated serious cardiac illness, which hospitalized me on our UK return. I was given days to live. Thanks to God, much prayer, and

---

25. *Don't Look Now*, 1973 film/DVD; dir. Nicholas Roeg, starring Julie Christie and Donald Sutherland.

great medical care, I survived—but our marriage did not. Fifteen months' convalescence, mandatory retirement, and the loss of our provided house all took their toll. We parted. My then wife with her salaried post (and index-linked pension) rightly used our capital to buy her future home, securing her way forward.

My pension kicked in, the denomination recommended me for a rental house, and I began rebuilding my sinking life without its various known compass points of the preceding thirty years. I downsized my life: broadcasting and conference-speaking, growing vegetables, preaching occasionally, joining a high school board. I began writing again seriously— poetry, theology, social policy, etc. My world totally changed—and had to. I relish this exciting, unforeseen, yet creative new life.

Just as Venice is a sinking city—it will be below the lagoon's waves within generations—so my life is a parable of the need for change. As we begin to consider the ecological impact of global warming, we realize how many other cities and communities may sink below the rising water levels. Ducats may have been replaced by gold standards, euros may have replaced some national currencies and one day perhaps the *yuan* will replace the dollar as globally dominant. The economic world has to totally change. Its former compass points, which evolved over generations, will soon no longer exist meaningfully. Westernized nations must downsize their lives, trajectories, and expectations. Our economic practices will have to be reforged because people and all living things matter more to God and this planet than any principles that advocate self-interested acquisition or enforced sharing.

Our traditional compass points may be gone. Westernized nations will have to downsize. We will not have what we once expected—we may lose homes, wealth, and livelihoods—but with creativity, the future can be even more exciting: "What lies at the heart of the Christian understanding of life in the Spirit: a different economic vision for God's household on earth."[26] Time is short and the water rises.

26. McFague, *Life Abundant*, 187.

ECOLOGY

4 Back to the Garden?

A few years ago, I went to an informal supper party, where a casually dressed, fascinating man described a recent experience from a business trip. He had been part of a small group who had traveled by minibus into a remote country area with hardly any inhabitants. It was summer and both plant and animal species were evident in their profusion amid birdsong. When the group got out of the vehicle, they were warned not to eat any berries or nuts, nor drink from a stream, but the raconteur claimed they were far too busy watching fearless foxes chase rabbits, and deer walk into the clearing where they stood. He was part of an intergovernmental delegation visiting the restricted lands around Chernobyl in Ukraine. After each stop, when they had taken their photographs and measurements, they took off their latex gloves, face masks, disposable overalls, and blue plastic forensic bootees as they climbed back into the minibus. All their protective clothing was then double-bagged for later incineration.

They passed decaying Soviet apartment blocks, abandoned playgrounds and vehicles in the remaining ghost towns. Once they stopped by an old wooden shack where an elderly couple had defied the authorities and had snuck back to their lifelong home, with its well water and vegetable garden. They claimed they knew that the land "might be sick," their water might be poisonous, and the vegetables they grew, just like the rabbits they trapped, might give them cancer—but "you have to die sometime." The saddest fact was that soldiers would prevent them leaving so they would never again see their relocated children and grandchildren. My supper-party acquaintance told his story through tears; his scientific detachment punctured by his very humanity.

I recount this in detail for it brings together the first two strands of our consideration—economy and ecology. Soviet (or anyone's) economic cheese paring has a planetary cost for generations to come if we do not invest properly for the sake of all.

Chernobyl, a small town near Pripyat in post-Soviet Ukraine, had suffered greatly during the Stalinist purges and had been chosen as a reparative site for a nuclear power station as part of an underfunded national initiative. In April 1986, Chernobyl's reactor no. 4 went into meltdown, killing some workers instantly but causing radiation sickness in its eponymous town and for 40,000 people in Pripyat, within thirty-six hours, before evacuation could take place. Quickly, a 30km-radius militarily administered exclusion zone was created. Within this seeming idyll, animals and birds have lost their natural fear of humans and thus seem to be more in profusion. But the incidence of mutant deformities is increasing, with greater percentages of albinism, sterility, insect gigantism, and smaller brain sizes noted in bird corpses. Imagine if breeding humans had remained . . . ?

Is there an environmental crisis?

I believe there is an environmental crisis, and over 95 percent of the world's scientists believe it too. They believe that we are undergoing significant climate change, as a result of the burning of fossil fuels that damages the ozone layer. Al Gore may have been a lot of things, and some say not quite right about every scientific theory, but his *An Inconvenient Truth*'s title says it all. The ecological crisis, facing Earth and all its species, is not just an inconvenient truth for industrialists and politicians, but an advancing and growing reality for everyone.

Environmental equals ecological. Too often, commentators talk about "damage to the environment" as though it is momentary, rather than pointing up the ecological costs of what has happened—or is happening! The globally infamous case of the 1984 gas explosion at the Union Carbide plant at Bhopal, India, highlights this. Although estimates of the death toll range from officially 2,700 to 16,000 in its immediate aftermath, over one million cases for personal injury compensation were registered with the Indian courts. Stillbirths rose 300 percent over the coming years for those who had inhaled the gas, while blindness, kidney disease, and various cancerous illnesses befell that and the next generation. Yet within days of the disaster, factory managers were claiming the toxic clouds had dispelled and the half-million local people had nothing to fear from this "short-term environmental incident" (as was later stated in court). The ecology of humans and other chordate species have all been affected by the Bhopal explosion. Science will be very hard pushed to say when, if ever, environmental does not equal ecological.

This chapter's introduction about the ecological disaster that has befallen Chernobyl tells of what can happen when human safeguards are not enough in the face of technological disaster. I am old enough to remember a childhood family holiday in southwestern England just after the *Torrey Canyon* disaster, which in 1967 was the world's greatest oil spillage. I recall getting oil globules on my feet on the shoreline, watching dead seabirds wash up each new morning, and listening to local children talk about how the fishing stocks had gone. Then in 1989, apologists try to diminish the five-times-larger spillage by *Exxon Valdez* in Prince William Sound, Alaska. Two years ago, my family revisited a town affected by the *Torrey Canyon* spillage, where a local shopkeeper reckoned that we are "almost back to rights after 1967's disaster": two whole generations! How long will it take for Prince William Sound? How many generations will suffer because of Chernobyl? Oh, did I forget to mention Fukushima in Japan . . . and how that will impact on the whole eastern Pacific Rim?

Regrettably, I could write a whole book briefly detailing such ecological disasters. That last word seems to be about the only one suitable for describing each instance. Some try to dismiss the *Torrey Canyon* and *Exxon Valdez* "moments" as part of the price for needing fossil fuels, or argue that we need factories like Bhopal's if we are to cheaply produce chemical pesticides, or say that we cannot have full nuclear safety so we must expect the Chernobyls and Fukushimas as part of the ecological cost of clean energy. Not so. There has yet to be one recorded fatality as a direct result of the failure of a Scottish, Canadian, or Scandinavian hydroelectric power plant. Yes, one day, someone will fly a light plane, helicopter, or glider mistakenly into a wind turbine—and there will be accidental loss of life. Renewable energy schemes may tragically cost some human lives without creating a multigenerational environmental disaster.

Climate change

But a far bigger crisis awaits, in that 95 percent of globally accreditable scientists know that climate change is occurring. Much of that is due to

the global warming, caused by CO2 emissions. We know the vast majority of this is humanly caused, by the excessive use of fossil fuels. There is
an Intergovernmental Panel on Climate Change (the IPCC), which from
2007 has produced a series of projections demonstrating what might occur
with each one degree centigrade rise of global temperatures. Unless urgent
(within a decade) action is taken, global temperatures will rise between
1.1°C and over 6°C;[1] these figures were originally deemed to have over
53 percent "correct probability" rising through 66 percent in 2015 towards
an expected 70 percent probability when this book is published (in 2017).
Planet Earth's peoples must stop creating "greenhouse gases" as soon as
possible. It is not just polar bears that will die if the polar icecaps melt, but
whole island groups will be submerged, their nations will be gone, and the
surviving people will become internationally homeless refugees. Complete
ecosystems and the biodiversity of several species will be lost—gone for-
ever! Time is short . . . and the waters are rising.

Two coinciding factors demonstrate the nature of climate change
caused by global warming. First, Arctic geographers can show an approxi-
mate summer diminution in the polar icecap of 50 percent between the
1970s and the 2000s. Canadian government marine ecologists have begun
accruing documentation (film, satellite tagging, Inuit testimony, etc.) of
the consequent summer invasion of orca pods, predating upon narwhal
primarily and beluga secondarily, since the 2010s. As the dominant alpha
marine predator, orcas are now in every global ocean, precisely because of
global warming and the loss of sea ice. Those same Arctic geographers are
also hearing from native Athabascan hunters, in both Alaska and western
Canada, of the loss of their traditional goose-hunting grounds as earlier
annual thaws are making those grounds inaccessible.

Second, that climate change is due to growing human abuse of the
planet. "Earth is home to millions of species . . . Just one dominates it.
Us. . . . And every one of these problems is accelerating as we continue to
grow towards a population of ten billion"[2]—so begins Stephen Emmott, the
head of UK's Computational Research Unit, in Cambridge, in his excellent
book, *Ten Billion*.

The bookshops' shelves are annually gaining more volumes, both
fictional and factual,[3] about what we are now having to face up to, eco-

1. Lynas, *Six Degrees*.

2. Emmott, *Ten Billion*, 2–7.

3. Monbiot, *Heat*.

logically. Just like other eco-activists, Christians must research, respond prophetically, and live within an "Earth-friendly" practical theology. As Emmott asserts, it means working harder in research, noting the verifiable links between various scientific research projects, which could not even be envisaged twenty years ago.

Biblical principles and Christian theology

Orthodox Christian theology affirms that the created order is good precisely because the Creator affirms it to be good. One does not have to believe in the inerrancy of the biblical allegories of creation, recorded in Genesis, to believe that there is a Creator, who may well be the divine wisdom that ordered creation from the scientists' Big Bang. However, the story told around Hebrew campfires for generations affirmed that God made the world and "saw that it was good"—repeatedly (Gen 1:31). Then someone wrote it all down on a scroll, ultimately naming it Genesis . . . and centuries later, some more folks decided that an inerrant, literalist view of Scripture is (falsely) the only credible viewpoint . . . landing the church with a whole heap of disgruntled believers, questioning students, and a queue of scientists on their way to the exit door.

Please wait. Throughout the horrible history of the Hebrews, involving murder, rape, war, genocide, and slavery, there was a love-hate relationship with this same Creator God, who continually called that same people back to peace, harmony, and community. God wanted them to be Israel—the "chosen people." God promised them a "land flowing with milk and honey" (Exod 3:8) if they would but heed God's direction, and journey under divine protection despite human adversity, accepting some basic rules called the Ten Commandments to give shape to a moral, community code (Exod 20:1–17; Deut 5:4–21). This story of God the Creator is confirmed by great hymns of praise, called Psalms, and behavioral guidance given by these same messenger of God, called prophets. Can you recognize the Hebrew Bible (sometimes called the Old Testament by Christians) in this paragraph?

It is hardly surprising that God's people had children like yours and mine, asking, "Where did we come from?" or "Who were the first people?" I could tell them all about *Australopithecus*, the findings at Kenya's Olduvai

Gorge,[4] and the African Exodus,[5] but they would not be satisfied with that. They wanted (and I needed) a "Once upon a time . . ." or "In the beginning . . ." narrative and that is what we have in Genesis. Helpfully, that goes on to show how God's representative humanity failed to live within the rules of Creation's idyllic garden (Eden, in Gen 3) and had to leave to begin their human wanderings and start learning from their mistakes. Just like my children!

In the introduction, I already rehearsed the Adam and Eve narrative as well as the ongoing journey of the Hebrew people into the nation which is now Israel. The rhythms of Jewish spirituality—Sabbath, sabbatical, jubilee[6]—all contribute towards that people's theological understanding of God's purposeful blessing of *shalom* in the peaceable indwelling of God-with-them in that blessed creation. That same understanding of God-with-us is at the heart of Christian incarnational theology as Jesus takes on our very humanity (Phil 2:3–14).

John 3:16 states that "God so loved the world, that he sent his Son . . ."; the "world" there is the cosmos—the universe and all that dwells therein—not yours nor my individualized, private existences. Jesus came that we "might have life in all its fullness" (John 10:10)—not a degrading planet where one in seven people live below the poverty line and another species becomes extinct every day. To live simply as Jesus did means that we exercise care for our environment, speak out against injustice, work as a renewed community, and serve our sisters and brothers. Now, that is God-with-us . . . but is it enough in the face of the coming ecological "tsunami"?

"Isms" and Gaia

Even Paul, the missionary evangelist, knew the Athenians to be "a godly lot" (Acts 17:22); they had a whole pantheon of gods. It was that Greek understanding that leads us to the concept of "polytheism," which means having belief in many gods.

As Christians, we have much to learn from Paul's psychology in not alienating his hearers then or ours now when we want to advance our arguments. Whether those are about Jesus' life-giving grace or a biblical understanding of creation demanding "Earth-friendly" discipleship, we do best

4. Leakey, *Origin of Humankind*.

5. Stringer and McKie, *African Exodus*.

6. Francis, *Shalom*, 20–23.

when we keep our listeners and conversation partners with us. We need to learn how to push against the world's opening doors . . .

Many Westernized folk close the doors to faith discussions, because they see faith as pantheistic—just a belief that an impersonal God is identical with all things—and reject such an impersonal God. From "pantheism," it is quite a small philosophical hop to believe that the divine is in everything. This is known as "panentheism" and is a prevalent belief system throughout the world. Its most common outworking is "animist" belief (from the Latin *anima* meaning "spirit" or "breath"; similar to the Hebrew *ruach*). Japanese Shintoism, East Asian (e.g., Malaya, Indonesia, Philippines), and many African and Western New Age beliefs are permeated with animism, just as the Nenet caribou herders' beliefs are.

Even the scientific world sees some merit in "quantum animism" where the mind, rather than the divine, permeates everything; possibly its most famous advocate is Stanford-educated Nick Herbert.[7] Anthropologists argue countervailing theories about some form of animism as providing the philosophical structure for a strong ecology. Christians can simply turn to biblical understandings of creation to understand that in a balanced doctrine of a Creator, we can see God-in-all-things but not necessarily God-*within*-all things.

Before moving on, we need to consider the Gaia Principle (sometimes known as its hypothesis or theory). This was devised by the NASA consultant James Lovelock, a chemist, while he was working on planetary modeling, and was named after Gaia, the Greek goddess of the Earth. Lovelock's thesis is that the whole biosphere controls the sustainability of life on Earth; therefore the Earth acts as one holistic "organism" interacting with its own atmosphere[8]—almost a biblical conception. However, Lovelock believes that global warming has already passed its tipping point and that life, as we know it, is no longer sustainable; and thus is heading towards its doomsday.[9] I disagree, believing Earth is still redeemable, finding myself sharing that view with scientists like the atheist Richard Dawkins.[10] But in our campaigning for "Earth-friendly" changes, many in the environmental/ecological lobby have swallowed Lovelock's Gaia Principle, whereas many in the scientific community have not. In prophetically challenging

7. Herbert, *Quantum Reality*.
8. Lovelock, *Gaia*.
9. Lovelock, *Vanishing Face of Gaia*.
10. Dawkins, *God Delusion*.

the world's politicians, we may be surprised at some of our co-travelers in wanting change.

Rio, Kyoto, Copenhagen, Paris: development goals and sustainable change

In 1992, the United Nations Conference on Environment and Development (UNCED) was held in Rio de Janeiro. Its "watershed" thinking about the planet's future caused it to be popularly known as the "Rio Summit." Of the 172 participating nations, 116 sent their heads of state—it was that important—while nearly 2,500 nongovernmental organizations (NGOs) attended. Four major issues among many were addressed:

- Commitment to alternative sources of energy to replace the use of fossil fuels;

- Commitment to scrutinize, then continually reduce to zero, the use of toxic chemicals and waste products (such as radioactive). Perhaps the UK government forgot this, Chernobyl, and Fukushima in their 2016 plans for more nuclear power plants?

- Commitment to creating greater reliance on new (forms of) public/mass transportation systems;

- Commitment to working together to combat the global scarcity of fresh drinking water.

Practically, all this resulted in global advocacy documents, such as *The Rio Declaration on Environment and Development* and "Agenda 21," a program of practical action which every US state, UK county, and Australasian province is meant to be utilizing. Recognition of this ongoing Agenda 21 "localization" is vital as churches together forge complementary responses and theology.

Clear critique could be offered in the failure of Rio's participant nature to "clean up their own backyards" environmentally or address the "causes of poverty." For example, one of the several Rio agreements, binding upon participant nations, was "not to carry out any activities on the lands of *indigenous peoples* that would cause *environmental degradation* or that would be culturally inappropriate." Perhaps the developing transnational, Gaz-Prom, has forgotten that in its dealings with the Nenet and their caribou.

But one important achievement is the Climate Change Convention Agreement, which led to the Kyoto Protocol.

Another important outworking of the Rio Summit was in the multinational production of the eight Millennium Developments Goals (commonly called MDGs).[11] This UN-led declaration set a broad-brush program of targets, which received differing levels of attention or response across the global majority of supportive nations. With hindsight, the goals about improving world health, infant mortality rates, and hunger issues fared much better in achieving measurable success (but still leaving much to be done), whereas the seventh MDG about environmental sustainability saw regression rather than progress.

Kyoto and Copenhagen

The Kyoto Protocol is a globally significant international treaty, bindingly made by 193 nations in Kyoto in 1997. It confirmed that:

1. Climate change was occurring;

2. Long-term, terminal global warming was ongoing; and

3. Man-made carbon dioxide emissions were its cause.

It committed signatory nations to reduce their greenhouse gas emissions significantly within declared time scales and caused the G7 nations to commit to programs for the eradication of all fossil fuel usage by 2030. Canada effectively withdrew from the Kyoto Protocols by the end of 2012. By the end of that same "commitment period," Japan and Russia failed to sign up to the protocol, while the official US and Chinese governments refused to ratify it *if* it was going to be deemed as legally binding. This flip-flop approach by leading world governments is both wrong and irresponsible. Quite simply, politicians do not want to the pay the price, whether electorally or by imposing taxation or creating national/federal legislation, to comply with Earth's need to reverse climate change. It will be the prophetic work of green/eco-activists as well as Christians to call their governments to account by demanding decisive "Earth-friendly" action.

Regrettably, the Copenhagen 2009 United Nations Climate Change Conference was shambolic as publicly nations prevaricated about the Kyoto Protocols, paying strong lip service to the need for climate change

11. www.unmillenniumdevelopmentproject.org/goals.

and greenhouse gas reduction. The annoyance of smaller developing world nations at the overconsuming Westernizing nations, including China, was palpable. Figures published in 2010 by the Church of Scotland demonstrate the discrepancy in carbon consumption because in the UK "We use 9.8 tonnes of carbon per person compared to 0.1 tonnes in Malawi and 20.6 in the USA."[12] To reduce our carbon usage and carbon emissions is to recognize the "log in our own eyes" rather than the splinter in others'. Tragically, Copenhagen 2009—as that summit became known—had almost every nation you can name "noting" the need for major reduction in the creation of carbon emissions and GHGs, but very few adopted action to support it.

Paris

By Paris 2015, because of the recent work of a variety of NGOs, nearly all nations had recognized that any more than a 2°C rise in global temperatures would spell death for the planet. Some nations, such as the Marshall Islands, face obliteration as sea levels rise to engulf them, while nations like Bangladesh will suffer more frequent, devastating flooding for similar reasons. Change is necessary—not least the rapid halt of the use of fossil fuels, like coal and oil. Government intervention is required to enable the subsidized and widespread introduction of renewable energy production. Sadly, detailed intergovernmental haggling went on long after we all came home from Paris.

Sustainable?

Alongside all this, the UN is undertaking admirable work in calling intergovernmental groups and research together to create seventeen "Sustainable Development Goals" (SDGs).[13] This is as a result of a strong international consultative process, which culminated in this series of 2015 statements, building upon work initiated at Rio 1992 and in the MDGs, about such subjects as food, cities, clean water, and mass transport. Importantly, those seventeen SDGs were published by the UN two months before the 2015 Paris Summit, creating a positive bulwark against that scientists, politicians, and theologians could set measurable goals for action and reflection.

12. Young, *Building Home*, quoted to me in an e-mail from the author.
13. www.sustainabledevelopment.un.org/?menu=1300.

Because of my already-published writings, I will be still leading seminars about food and eco-developments throughout 2016/17 into 2018 (and beyond) at SDG conferences. It will be for readers to individually take and "earth" those SDGs, as part of your own nation's as well as a global education process, to encourage both ourselves and others to take seriously the threat of climate change.

Dominion, domination, and human pride

One of the key biblical concepts in its theology of creation is that of dominion. This means humankind has both responsibilities and rights for that very creation. It is about respect, care, and stewardship, as I expanded upon in my previous book, *What in God's Name Are You Eating?*[14] We can quickly understand that if in our everyday diet we consider sourcing as much as possible of our food locally and in season, buying meat, dairy products, and eggs only from places where free-range conditions, organic feedstuffs, and humane slaughter are normative practices. Westernized consumers seem to have far more problems in applying those good *and* Christian qualities of care, respect, and stewardship to the rest of our lives.

Every mile we drive creates carbon emissions. Using either air-con or central heating creates carbon emission; what is wrong with opening a window or putting on an extra sweater while you get the house reinsulated? Everything has a carbon footprint: from bananas to brain surgery, from coffee to cars, from washing machines to weapons.[15]

If Christians really respect and honor God as Creator, we are called to respect and care for creation as stewards. We cannot go down to the mall and order up another planet for when our human abuse has exhausted the resources, which God has entrusted not just to us but to everyone made in that divine image as well as the rest of the created taxonomy of species. We, or at least Western nations, live with an attitude of such human domination that we fantasize that we can undertake such a mall journey, rather than practically exercise one of increasingly biblically inspired dominion.

As the green activist Jonathan Porritt has written: "One of the most crucial tasks for Christians today is therefore to reinterpret the meaning of 'dominion' in terms of stewardship and ecological responsibility for life

14. Francis, *What in God's Name*, 41–46.
15. Berners-Lee, *How Bad are Bananas.*

on Earth."[16] But such theological questions must be continually reforged. In his 2006 Sarum Lectures, Richard Bauckham openly tested his thesis that traditional views of "stewardship" are now "inadequate" and that we must now understand ourselves to be a constituent part of a "community of creation."[17]

Domination is never right

One of the best and worst examples of human domination took place in 2015. The crossbow-shooting of a dynastic Zimbabwean lion by a Minnesotan dentist made global headlines and went viral on the Internet, with the details of how the lion was enticed from his protected reserve by accomplices of this serial hunter. He had also shot endangered rhino and leopard. The best place for a rhino's horn is on its living head and not on a rich American's wall nor, in a Chinese apothecary (where it has no medical efficacy!). Trophy hunting serves no moral purpose, is selfish, endangers important species' bloodlines, and deserves both condemnation and punitive reparation.

Yet it is not that many generations since white people believed they had the right to make their black sisters and brothers into slaves—a dreadful form of domination. Many Americans, Russians, Chinese, Europeans, and others believe the best way to run the world is by threat and violence. This is an institutionalized form of domination that is entirely counter to the biblical trajectory and God-in-Jesus, who came that *all* might have "life in all its fullness" and taught his followers to "turn the other cheek"[18] (Luke 6:29). Domination is anti-Christian—God-trusting dominion is the biblical model.

You may have already worked me out. But that incident with Adam, Eve, and a certain apple was about domination. True dominion would have meant heeding God's way and leaving that tree and its fruit well alone. But no, Adam and Eve thought they knew better. They did not. Did they not already have enough in the garden? It is tempting to ask, after both *Torrey Canyon* and *Exxon Valdez*, did anybody notice the missing fossil fuel, apart from the damaged shorelines and dying seabirds? After Chernobyl

16. Porritt, *Seeing Green*, 209.

17. Bauckham, *Bible and Ecology*.

18. Francis, *Shalom*, 138–48.

or Fukushima, did anybody notice there was not enough power for those nations (there was!)?

To think we can dominate Planet Earth for our own selfishness is not biblical dominion; it is human greed, driven by our pride to dominate rather than share God's gifts as Jesus invites us to. Simply, it is a failure to understand ourselves as part of God's "community of creation."

Turn around . . .

There is a Hebrew proverb: "pride goes before a fall" (Prov 16:18). It certainly did for Adam and Eve. How did it feel for those cleaning up globally known oil spillages or nuclear meltdowns? We cannot lose our past but we can realize what is happening now. We can choose to say our past priorities have dominated and our present behaviors must change. President Obama's brave 2015 call to the USA to grossly cut its carbon emissions recognizes the human arrogance that wants domination over the world that it has marred, not made.[19]

Can we restore Eden?

The simple answer is "No." We cannot get back to a garden of Eden. *Jurassic Park* scenarios inform us that we cannot package nor re-create a world as it once was. Equally, we cannot redesign the planet from what it once was. As an illustration of that, we can quickly become aware of the problems of so-called "invasive species."

Invasive species

These are animal or plant species that are introduced into a nonnative habitat, where often they become at best a pest or at worst a threat to other native species and often consequently to their new environment.

One of the best global examples is *myocastor coypus*, better known in north America and Europe as "nutria"[20] and elsewhere as the coypu. Originally from South America, these large herbivorous rodents are

19. Obama, *Audacity of Hope*, 168.

20. In Latin or Spanish-speaking countries, the word "nutria" refers to the otter, hence "coypu."

predominantly aquatic, living in freshwater wetland. They eat and breed prodigiously, destroying their surrounding habitat before moving on. Imported for breeding on fur farms, escapees and/or released animals caused havoc. Brought into Louisiana in the 1930s, then the Chesapeake Bay area of Maryland, sufficient problems occurred within decades to require state legislative controls and eradication programmes in both states by the early 2000s. If one considers that Louisiana loses wetland the size of a football field each and every hour (feral hogs and other factors also contribute to this), the alarming spread of nutria/coypu to other states as far apart as Oregon, California, and the Carolinas is not comforting. It is little wonder that the UK began an eradication process, supposedly completed in 1989, and that in 1996, New Zealand declared *Myocastor coypus* a "prohibited species."

Because of its geographic isolation and nonindigenous colonization, Australia often introduced species for a particular purpose—only recognizing later how this had become "invasive." Five Australian examples provide fascinating case studies:

1. The 1930s importation of the cane toad (*Bufo marinus*) by the Australian Sugar Corporation to control, by eating, the destructive cane beetle is frightening. Cane toads' bodies contain toxins that kill the toads' predators, such as goannas (large lizards), who quickly suffer nonviable falls in population while the cane toads multiply exponentially. The resultant loss of goanna numbers in northern Australia means they are simply not there to also eat saltwater crocodile eggs—part of their natural diet—meaning that "salties" are growing in (human–life-threatening) numbers.

2. The stupid introduction of the European rabbit, simply for hunting by humans for sport or food, has led to an explosive growth in rabbit numbers, severe habitat loss, and the costly erection of continent-wide "rabbit-proof fences."

3. The nineteenth-century importation of dromedaries from India and horses from South Africa and Europe has led to many animals becoming feral "brumbies," all causing erosive habitat loss.

4. The 1850s importation of Indonesian water buffalo, for meat, milk, and ploughing, with escapees becoming wild, has led to the destruction of water courses (the buffaloes' natural wallow) and many plant species.

5. The bringing in of the giant mimosa (*mimosa pigra* and associated subspecies), from central America, has squeezed out many native plants, due to the easy spread and height of this leguminous shrub. The Australian government legislatively declared it to be a "noxious weed," requiring control if not eradication.

We return (below) to the implications of such human mismanagement of balanced environments.

Different regions have different problems. The mountain lion or cougar has a habitat extending throughout the Americas, despite national boundaries, with territories ranging from mountain regions, through forest, to desert- or plains-edge. Although local residents may rail against incoming cougar habitats, this is *not* invasive but simply a matter of "territory expansions"; a known zoological phenomenon. Reasoned Christian thinking/theology must take account of scientific differentiation between such "territory expansion" and invasive species when making public statements.

The introduction from North America of the American or signal crayfish (*Pacifastacus leniusculus*) and Canada geese (*Branta canadensis*) to British freshwaters required different responses. As in other European countries, the signal crayfish ousted native species into virtual extinction, forcing the lesson that if a habitat is not easily controlled (such as rivers), the introduction of new nonnative species *must* be totally avoided. However, if a species can be culled humanely in numbers, such as by aerial shooting, the risks of species introduction (e.g., Canada geese) *can* be considered alongside the threat to native competing species. What was jointly learned and accepted was that an alpha predator (i.e., with no natural enemies) or a keystone herbivore (i.e., with few natural predators) *should not* be introduced without safeguards for realistic, regular culling and its humane practice.

An associated question with "invasive species" is the principle of "re-wilding."[21] This is when controlled scientific reintroductions of now-extinct-from-that-region species occur. The next chapter's opening illustration about how wolves are now threatening the Wyoming populations of cougar is a good example. In Britain, we have enough problems with escaped/reintroduced wild boar to recognize that to reintroduce alpha predators such as brown bears is madness, whereas the currently controlled reintroduction of the once-native European lynx is not.

21. Monbiot, *Feral.*

Christians have huge prophetic responsibility to consider what this "dominion" issue means, in relation to both "invasive species" and "re-wilding" issues. If anyone is uncertain of that, consider the introduction of *Fallopia japonica*, more commonly known as Japanese knotweed, into Britain and North America, where 80 percent of US states and all but two Canadian provinces are adversely affected by this fast-growing herbaceous perennial, which eats through concrete and roads, destroys homes, and overruns habitats.

More fundamentalist Christians will regard "invasive species" or "re-wilding" as "messing with God's creation," whereas more scientifically oriented thinkers will recognize the folly of wrongly introduced taxonomic species.

Lagom *for creation*

It will take many generations for the Chernobyl region to recover—if it ever can. Because of the proximity of the ocean and global tide patterns, it is almost impossible scientifically to assess whether Fukushima will have caused lasting environmental damage. Perhaps the regions and surrounding oceans can recover from *Torrey Canyon* or *Exxon Valdez* oil spillages within a few generations. The genetic fallout from the Bhopal disaster continues as do those from 1945's nuclear devastation at Hiroshima and Nagasaki. But how long can the world's people afford to take these risks with the planet?

We cannot replace the keynote species or biospheres if we continue to want palm oil via creating plantations of it across southeast Asia. The same is true for illegal and multinationally demanded logging in the Amazon basin or cattle ranching in the Pantanal for western burger outlets across the globe. We have to change our demands, which are killing the planet. *Lagom* as a global principle is needed in all things.

We have to begin conducting our global commercial activity with different priorities. "Instead of investing mainly in sawmills, fishing boats, and refineries, development should now focus on reforestation, restocking of fish populations, and renewable substitutes for dwindling reserves of petroleum. The latter should include investment in energy efficiency, since it is impossible to restock petroleum deposits."[22] All these are principles that the Shetland Islands Council have already adopted (41–43).

22. Costanza, ed., *Introduction to Ecological Economics*, 88.

And so . . .

If we are to get back to the garden, we must learn from Adam and Eve, the Bible, Jesus, and a world of science that is telling us that all in the garden now is not so rosy.

5 A Theology of God-Envisioned, "Earth-Friendly" Stewardship

Most North American readers will be aware of the warnings issued to both rural town residents and mountain hikers about the mountain lion or cougar. However, the work of the internationally attested Teton Cougar Project, based just north of Jackson, Wyoming, has changed the thinking of wildlife ecologists about this species.[1] Although cougars have previously been assumed to be solitary, marauding alpha predators, the Teton project has documentary evidence (radio-tracking, static camera footage, and field study) that cougars are social animals, with adults conglomerating, or even nursing females sharing their kill with both cubs and roaming males without aggression. However, during the ten-year life of the project, the number of wild cougars has halved because of both hunting by humans and the reintroduction of wolves into that area of Wyoming. While strong arguments remain for "re-wilding" (see chapter 4), there must be serious question whether either the federal or state game and fish departments should ever be majority-funded by residents buying hunting licenses. If we want cougars (or whatever species is under threat), we have to stop killing them.

Good prophetic theology will challenge economic or human or ecological practices that damage biospheres and constituent species. Christians need to take the best attestable scientific knowledge when helping communities determine what is a balanced "Earth-friendly theology."

---

1. www.panthera.org/node/32.

Not just voices from the margins?

Just as the Teton Cougar Project reveals, we need quality and accountable science to support the voices for change. When such US establishment figures as Al Gore (54) and Barack Obama (65), are effectively saying, "Enough is enough, we must change and turn around . . ." it is time to do so. And now Pope Francis has joined in.

The environmental lobby

In North America, the writings of Thoreau established a pattern of "nature writing."[2] Nearly a century later, the work of natural philosophers, such as Cambridge literature lecturer John Stewart Collis,[3] established "lay voices" as legitimate commentators in the need to preserve the planet. "Whenever any species oversteps the mark in numbers or behaviour, it pays the penalty and meets with catastrophe."[4]

I was a high school student, majoring in science, when I first read US government scientist Rachel Carson's *Silent Spring*, foretelling the silence of the birds and such a global catastrophe because of human intervention. Her book detailed how the unbridled use of pesticides was damaging co-species, causing mammalian cancers and the decline of avian species. She called for statutory restriction. Her work led to the USDA ban on DDT, which is now spreading across the world.

The research work of the Chennai-based M. S. Swaminathan provided the impetus and lead that enabled India to reach agricultural self-sufficiency in the 1970s. This allowed India to become the world's second largest producer of sugar and rice. But the resultant international trade, which India's rising population and burgeoning economy creates, threatens to pull it away from such "food security."[5] Initially goaded by 1943's Bengali famine, and inspired by Gandhi and the struggle for independence, Swaminathan became a plant geneticist, who worked with succeeding Indian governments and key politicians, to create a nutritional "food security" for all citizens, based on three principles:

2. Thoreau, *Walden and Other Writings*.
3. Collis, *Down to Earth*.
4. Collis, *Vision of Glory*, 199.
5. Swaminathan, *Science and Sustainable Food Security*.

1. Global nutritional security should be our new goal, based upon self-sufficient nations bartering their surplus; this integrated approach would create "Earth-friendly" diets and gradually eradicate global hunger or famine.

2. Work should be directed towards globally needed state-funded science programs—whether in the exploration of genetically modified foods, alternative energy sources, or biosphere and species preservation.

3. The preservation of biodiversity is vital for maintaining plant species, including crop varieties and potential medications, and animal bloodlines.

The latter was practically emphasized in Swaminathan's advocative leadership and the successive Indian government's commitment to the Lutheran Church-inspired Svalbard Vault (a global seed bank and animal gene store) overseen and maintained by the prophetically thinking Norwegian government.

In North America, Pete Seeger (1919–2014), the peace activist, environmental campaigner, and folk singer, wrote songs that have become standards, such as "If I Had a Hammer." He spent part of his life living on *Clearwater*, a sloop on the Hudson River, protesting about pollution of that waterway by transnational corporations. Later, Joni Mitchell, with songs like "Big Yellow Taxi" and "Woodstock," created anthems for my generation, who wanted pesticide-free food and to get "back to the garden."

In Australia, Vivienne Elanta (1951–2004) became involved in the "deep ecology" movement and was a pioneering inspiration to younger green/eco-politicians, who now serve in NGOs or state governance. With others, she campaigned extensively for the preservation of total biospheres, not just flagship species. She cofounded Greens Western Australia and the Australian Gaia Foundation. Like Swaminathan, she saw that the preservation of regional, and therefore global, biodiversities was key to planetary and human survival.

In Britain, writer-speakers such as Jonathan Porritt[6] and Tony Juniper[7] worked for environmental organizations like Friends of the Earth, stood for Green Party policies and now act as eco-advisers to many Stock Exchange-listed companies. Within the Green Party, Caroline Lucas, an NGO

---

6. Porritt, *Seeing Green.*

7. Juniper, *Saving Planet Earth.*

adviser,[8] and Molly Scott Cato,[9] an economist, both found electoral support to represent UK constituencies at Westminster and Strasbourg respectively.

The point is that these voices were worldwide. Initially these advocates were standing outside the mainstream protection of corporate employers and became committed to global environmentalism by conviction and experience. What is noticeable is that their voices do not remain marginalized as both governments and people recognize the wisdom of their research.

Scott Cato, a Quaker as well as an internationally respected economist, writes:

> In an era of climate change and economic crisis it becomes clearer every day that human society needs to undertake a rapid and radical transition to a new paradigm for social and economic life . . . . We are in times of crisis and times when dramatic, if not revolutionary change is called for. Beset by financial and ecological crises it is clear that the human race is threatened, that the dominant global model of the economy is broken and that we have taken a wrong turning.[10]

Now that is what I call prophecy and it demands some Earth-friendly theological advocacy in response.

An Olympic effort

After the Olympic Games of summer 1976 virtually bankrupted Montreal, sustainability questions increasingly dominated planning for the games. Atlanta's revitalization of a brownfield site in 1996, creating facilities with a different long-term usage, set a benchmark for the future. London 2012 again used a brownfield site, de-polluting local rivers and creating better mass-transit systems and long-term housing projects in its aim to be the "world's first truly sustainable Olympic Games."

Rio's successful bid for the 2016 games was predicated upon "A Green Games for a Blue Planet." Brazil already sourced 45 percent of their energy needs from renewable sources. They were hoping to power all Rio's buses by 2016 on locally produced ethanol (or biodiesel); a fact awaiting verification. Sadly, crime and the threat of kidnapping thwarted the use of a new

---

8. Woodin and Lucas, *Green Alternatives to Globalisation*.

9. Scott Cato, *Green Economics*.

10. Scott Cato, "Turning the World Upside Down," 43–44.

cycling network linking all the Olympic sites just as human pollution still blighted the sailing and rowing venues, as well as other parts of Rio's amazing shoreline.

Like the Olympics, theology must live with the reality of human failings yet remain exemplary under the world's gaze. Like the Olympics, theology is both a big and global project. It has to aim high, be visionary, setting goals and agenda for the whole planet—not just for a tiny community of fearful Christians, hiding in their meeting together. Like the Olympics, theology will always have the need for fresh thinking, which is sustainably resourceful and practical.

Towards an "Earth-friendly" theology

When I was child, I loved to watch a local blacksmith heat metal and hammer it into a useful shape on an anvil. As an adult, I became a potter and if a hand-thrown pot dried to become irregular, unstable, or potentially unusable, I would crumble it then use the rehydrated clay. Theology is like this. It needs to be forged and hammered into useful shape. But if it becomes an unworkable vessel, it needs crumbling before reworking. That is why I like to work "towards a theology" because it will be perennially not quite finished, demanding critique and requiring further work.

Sources

Rooted in both Celtic spirituality and the work of medieval mystics such as Meister Eckhart, contemporary "green" or eco-theology has three dominant sources: within the Catholic tradition, the Anabaptist–Mennonite stream and the work of ecofeminists. I used the ninth chapter of my 2016 book, *Shalom: The Jesus Manifesto*,[11] to detail and analyze that threefold development more fully than space allows here.

It is also important to acknowledge the stance of Orthodox Churches in affirming a strong Creator-creation theology but (regrettably) they are only just producing more written theology.[12] "Human redemption can be only understood as an integral part of the redemption of the whole

---

11. Francis, *Shalom*, 106–16.
12. Chryssavgis and Foltz, eds., *Toward an Ecology of Transfiguration*.

creation."[13] That statement alongside, Charles Birch's call at the 1975 Nai-
robi World Council of Churches—"The rich must live more simply so that
the poor can simply live"—are two principles for the forging of an eco- or
"Earth-theology."

Whether in historic Franciscan theology[14] or contemporarily the
unorthodox thinking of the former Dominican, Matthew Fox,[15] or the
orthodox academe of Celia Deane Drummond,[16] the Roman Catholic tradition helped establish eco-theology. It found strong support from South
American liberation theologians: "The challenge is to make people see one
another as members of a great earthly family together with other species
and find their way back to the community of other living beings, the planetary and cosmic community."[17] Perhaps the greatest imprimatur was Pope
Francis's *Laudato Si'* encyclical,[18] which emphasized the centrality of eco-
theology, and was aimed just as much at the world's peoples as the church
ecumenically. Pope Francis declared: "We are not facing two crises, one
environmental and the other social, but rather one complex crisis, which is
both social and environmental. Strategies for action demand an integrated
approach."[19] I am already grateful to several Roman Catholic contexts for
invitations to discuss this book's thesis and application, in the light of that
papal encyclical.

Historically, the Anabaptist movement is rooted within transient
groups, which found safety in community and increasingly rural exile.
Whether that is in their early (post-Reformation) escape to become (im)
migrant land workers in eastern Europe, or last century's Amish farming
neighborhoods or Bruderhof communities escaping from Nazis to South
America, "living lightly" upon and caring for the land, are increasing theological hallmarks.[20] A contemporary Anabaptist educator writes: "We are
to serve wild nature in a way that not only enables it to flourish but also to
achieve its full potential in God."[21] The whole movement is permeated with

---

13. Gregorios, "New Testament Foundations for Understanding Creation," 89.

14. Ramon, *Franciscan Spirituality*, 126–36.

15. Fox, *Original Blessing*.

16. Deane-Drummond, *Eco-Theology*.

17. Boff and Elizondo, *Ecology and Poverty*, 88.

18. Francis, *Laudato Si'*.

19. Ibid., para. 139, 70.

20. Francis, *Anabaptism*.

21. Moules, *Fingerprints of Fire*, 85.

a "living lightly upon the land" practical theology[22] and economic practices which are nonexploitative and avoid usury.[23]

Many highly respected feminist theologians have evolved into eco-theologians, seeing their politicization extending to speak for all species and the planet and not just gender dichotomies. "It was based on an unbiblical and humanly wrong pattern of domination, exercised oppressively and imperialistically."[24] I have been heavily influenced by Rosemary Radford Ruether,[25] Dorothee Soelle,[26] and Sallie McFague.[27] McFague calls attent to "the recognition that God is with us, not only embodied in Jesus of Nazareth but in all of nature, thus uniting creation and sanctifying bodily life; and finally, the promise of a renewed creation through the hope of resurrection, a promise that includes the entire cosmos and speaks to our ecological despair . . . ."[28] It may seem politically incorrect but I believe the childbearing capacity of women gives them an innate ability to see a more balanced vision for their children's future: "To bless the children means to leave the trees standing for them."[29] The future of this planet, our co-species, and our children depends upon our praxis now.

What we need is to take the paths taken by historic Christianity, be it Celtic, Orthodox, mystical, or Franciscan, then look at the signposts which contemporary eco-theologians are offering to us. Reforging them as our own, both as a practical agenda and a prayerful spirituality, will create an "Earth-friendly" discipleship.

Signposts

All these can be summarized as developing eco-theology, involving the following principles:

- There is a holistic biblical vision of God's creation, beginning with the Genesis narratives, affirming Jesus-style discipleship that reflects

22. Longacre, *Living More with Less.*

23. Kraybill and Nolt, *Amish Enterprise.*

24. Francis, *Dorothee Soelle,* 79.

25. Ruether, *Gaia and God.*

26. Soelle, with Cloyes, *To Work and to Love.*

27. McFague, *New Climate for Theology.*

28. McFague, *Life Abundant,* 166.

29. Soelle, *Theology for Sceptics,* 92.

care for the planet, culminating in Revelation's conviction that God's purpose will be revealed in a city, where the river of life flows and trees grow. It is vital to recognize the interweaving of Hebrew-based theology with "the land."[30]

- It is built upon the biblical understandings of dominion and steward-ship rather than human-centered domination: "If we understand our-selves as lords and owners of the earth and act as though we still had a second earth at our disposal—if we deny our creatureliness—then for us creation is merely usable material."[31]

- In the writings of the New Testament church, we find a growing af-firmation of the "new earth-new creation" construct. Paul reminds the Corinthian church that Christians are called to be in the vanguard of God's new creation (2 Cor 5:17). Revelation envisions the "new heaven and a new earth." Today, the church needs prophetically to state why: "New creation is not just for individuals, it also impacts on us, and through us, as a community. As the Church, we are the body of Christ and so collectively we are the new creation. We demonstrate that new creation in all that we do and in the way that we are people in society."[32]

- A recognition that humankind through its actions (economic, eco-logical, and as nations) and reflection will determine whether "we" limit Earth's God-given purpose and destiny. As former Archbishop of Canterbury Rowan Williams stated: "Something about the way God leads us through history is linked, it seems, with our growth towards a situation in which we take a more and more creative role in shaping our environment."[33]

- Rethinking past values; this will mean not only rejecting the domi-nation model but also reworking the dominion motif, as well as traditional theological assumptions. "To begin to define an ethic for ecological living, we need to revisit the questions of good and evil, sin and fallenness."[34] Think Adam, Eve, and the apple—how should we challenge our stereotypism?

30. Brueggemann, *Land*.
31. Soelle, *Thinking about God*, 48.
32. Hodson and Hodson, "Climate Justice," 137.
33. Williams, "Urbanisation, the Christian Church and the Human Project," 15.
34. Ruether, *Gaia and God*, 255.

- Respect and responsibility are needed. "It is about responsible earth stewardship as well as responsible person stewardship. Eco-justice is what Jesus was about . . . when he recommended and practised a simple lifestyle."[35] It is about respecting the creation that God has entrusted to *our* care.

- Ecology must affect our lifestyle both as churches and individuals: "Ecology is not just a mark of mission but a mark of discipleship."[36]

- Good theology is based in sound research. For example, although the present green lobby is raising important questions about "fracking" (hydro-pressured shale-gas extraction), we must recognize that it has been undertaken since the 1940s in the USA and the 1960s in Britain. Therefore the key questions *now* must center around its growing commercialism, its proportionality, the safety and bio-security of both environments and all local species (including humans!), etc.

These should be enough to begin our discussion of key theological factors to affirm that God the Creator's pronouncement in the Genesis narrative is right: "God saw what was made and it was good" (Gen 1:31). Why destroy something that is good—unless one is a petulant and spoiled child? God has made us his heirs (Rom. 8:15ff.) and cocreators. There is a consistent biblical vision of the goodness of creation and human responsibility in its ongoing re-creation.

My hope is that you and a group of trusted friends (not all need be Christians) can sit together over time, for prayer, study, and several meals, taking these expressions of faith as I perceive them and reforging them as a working theology for your context. "[The] work of social and ecological witness is necessarily about protest. Theologically speaking, this makes it prophetic."[37] Whether others see us as protesters or prophets may depend upon the social humanity of our gathering together as well as the work and theology forged.

---

35. Meyer and Meyer, *Earthkeepers*, 33.

36. Deane-Drummond, *Eco-Theology*, 181.

37. McIntosh, *Soil and Soul*, 121.

Praxis, partners, and purpose

Community, congregational, and personal discipleship must become a praxis—an ongoing "cycle" of prayerful action and active reflection. I question whether it can be cyclical because that could leave us in a static circle of introspection. Hence the joke about the last seven words of the church: "We've never done it like that before!" I believe praxis must be helical, gently progressing forward, prayerfully noting our past points of reflection and research while learning the lessons from the failures and sins of our past actions, improving, encouraging, and honing our ongoing Jesus-shaped discipleship.

Although I will say much more about inter-human relations in the Ecumeny section, it is important to note here that our ecological activism will need to be undertaken with others, whether they share our faith, practice another, or are agnostic. It seems to me that we cannot afford to be anonymous Christians—we need to offer praise when praise is due. Clearly, our everyday "walk with God" personally requires contemplative prayer and Bible study. Our shared action with others can receive blessing in shared meals or prayer times with a few others and thanksgiving to God in worship. But we also need to applaud secular or civic initiatives that enrich and improve our world and its environments *and* say why as Christians we believe them to be so important. Equally, when we work with others, whether it is clearing a neighborhood swale or running a fair-trade market stall, when questioned we need to be prepared to say, "Yes, I follow Jesus," without threat or allowing anything more than our behavior and lifestyle to witness to that truth.

The magisterial Reformers declared that the chief aim of all humankind is to glorify God. As we work to honor the wonder, beauty, and diversity of Creator God's handiwork, we glorify the Creator who reveals even more in the Savior, Jesus, who came that we might "have life in all its fullness" (John 10:10). Our purpose in this earthly life is to glorify the God whom we acknowledge, that others might share that fullness of life.

It was Sarah Werner, who researches Mennonite environmental initiatives, who alerted me afresh to the writings of Norman Wirzba: "An appreciation for the doctrine of creation will lead to a meaningful, wholesome reconnection with the wider social, ecological, cosmological and divine contexts in which we now live."[38] Our interrelationship is not just with the

38. Wirzba, *Paradise of God*, 2.

creation but the Creator too, as well as the creatures with whom we share the planet. This calls us to live responsibly in an "Earth-friendly" way. Then:

> We will discover that the Creation is not in any sense indepen-
> dent of the Creator, the result of a primal creative act, long over
> and done with but is the continuous, constant participation of all
> creatures in the being of God . . . . We will discover that for these
> reasons our destruction of nature is not just bad stewardship, or
> stupid economics, or a betrayal of family responsibility; it is the
> most horrid blasphemy.[39]

I now have reduced the public appearances of my "Save Trees—Eat More Beavers" T-shirt to my backyard workdays because if we manage the planet properly, both trees and beavers will find their ecological balance. That rather simple example exemplifies what we must do on every level: let the earth find its balance to thrive, without undue human interference and destruction, while we reuse what was once part of our consumerist lifestyle. That is why the next chapter contains ten action points for us all to pursue. Then God's vision for "a new heaven and a new earth" (Rev 21:1) may yet come to pass.

---

39. Berry, *Art of the Commonplace*, 308.

6 Making the Practical Changes—
Ten Ways to Make a Real Difference

Commit to zero deforestation

One of the planet's greatest problems is deforestation. Basic biology tells us that trees and algae "process" carbon dioxide, releasing oxygen into the atmosphere. More trees and forests can help create a healthier planet.

Three main deforestation problems exist. One is uncontrolled logging in the Amazon basin, as well as Indonesia and other Asian forests, contributing to those three problems:

1. Deforestation destroys biodiversity, through the nonsustainable extraction of various woods for Westernized usage, including "exclusive furniture" (as the advertisers term it).

2. That cleared land is often used for cash monocropping (thus leaching the soil into aridity) or surface mining or ranching cheap beef for North American burger chains.

3. The clearance of Asian forests for palm oil plantations and production, which could still become the most threatening.

We need to use our power as consumers and/or shareholders (who does your pension fund invest in?) to change policies and practices to save the planet. Ecumenical action across cities can challenge manufacturers and resource processors in their towns, just as denominations can challenge banks and pension funds. Mobilize!

Many Westernized foodstuffs, toiletries, cosmetics, and soaps contain palm oil (just as whale oil was used a century ago!) and these products are just the well-known the tip of an ecologically disastrous iceberg, which is destroying habitats and complete species. In southeast Asia, rainforests are being systematically cleared to make way for palm oil producing plantations. Such plantations cannot sustain populations of indigenous species (such as orangutans, many native plants, and keystone herbivores) and destroy the ozone production levels of a rainforest. By 2012, a tide began to turn. In 2013, the world's second largest pulp and paper producer, Indonesia's Asia Pulp and Paper, announced an immediate ban on further rainforest clearing.

Shortly after, Wilmar, the world's largest palm oil producer, announced that "at least 45 percent" of its production would be achieved by zero deforestation; but what does this mean and is it enough? When, by 2014, US household brands such as Cargill, Colgate-Palmolive, Ferrero, Mars, and Proctor & Gamble had made similar zero-deforestation commitments, we must applaud, monitor, but still buy fewer palm oil products—just look on the ingredients list. To help you further, you can download (from the Internet) a list of companies that use only "certified sustainable palm oil," and are thus committed to zero deforestation.

Decrease reliance on finite resources and fossil fuels[1]

We need to learn to eat seasonal, locally produced fruit and vegetables, not only to decrease global food miles, but also avoid buying from local "hothouse production" of such foods, which can be more environmentally damaging than food-mile abuses. We need to change our lives, reducing our energy consumption, taking fewer baths—"Rip out the tub (use it for backyard production of ducks!), install a shower"—and driving/flying a lot less.

To drive for two hours less per year does more environmental good than always taking your main TV off standby for a year; you *should* do both. Remember that one hot bath adds more to your carbon footprint than simply leaving your phone charger plugged in for a year; stop doing both. Take the train or use mass transport. Cycle to your grocery store every two days rather than driving to the mall weekly. As more "big box"

1. Berners-Lee and Clark, *Burning Question.*

stores sell Photo-Voltaic cells (PVIs) increasingly often and inexpensively, reduce your "on-grid" reliance and use "solar energy capture" instead.

We need to learn from Scandinavia, Canada, and sub-Arctic states and properly insulate our houses from heat loss while creating good ventilation for summer cooling. Turn off your air-con; one small PVI can power a desk fan. When attending Princeton's doctoral summer schools, I turned off my room's air conditioning, opened the windows, put up homemade fly-screens, and slept under a sheet; adapt! Externally cladding a house with fast-growing, locally produced larch (rather than slow-growing oak), which requires no oil-based preservative, can create a large decrease in energy consumption.

Any of us who have lived in city brownstone apartments, Parisian Haussmann buildings, midtown row (UK=terraced), or Scottish tenements know how much energy is saved by sharing hallways, party walls, and neighboring dwellings. All these buildings easily adapt to external cladding, rooftop wind turbines, and PVIs; funded by each building's residents, these can prophetically speak to city planners, and neighbors, while reducing residents' energy costs and reliance on fossil fuel. This is far more effective than creating great swathes of high-consumption detached suburban homes, where "everyone drives everywhere." Downsize your home and thus reduce your energy needs. Downsize your home to be nearer to your work or office. Go by bike—most Silicon Valley companies in California now provide as many bike racks as car park spaces.

Follow the example of Funen, Denmark, where individual local households together funded building a wind farm, paying for multiple turbines and an annual maintenance charge, in exchange for an 80 percent cheaper electricity supply. By 2015, Europe-wide mass media were reporting upon Ireland's progress in making changes like these. Ireland was producing between 25 and 33 percent of its electrical power needs from wind farms. This has been achieved without great political struggle or tax breaks, as well as with a population willing to accept the necessary landscape changes.

Challenge both your government and energy supplier to change the way they create and supply your energy.

Education—do your research

Christians, including theologians and pastors, must adopt the political mantra "education, education, education!" We must educate ourselves properly to offer sensible and coherent solutions into the debates which the *oikos* agenda generates, whether that is economically, ecologically, or ecumenically. This is not just about trotting out biblical quotes, or examples of a single, tiny congregation's downshift. We have to know how to paint the bigger picture. We need to use those broad brushstrokes in both conversation with friends or public discussion.

This is why at least one chapter in each of this book's sections attempts to exemplify such broad-brush narratives to provide the factual background for the development of vision and planning for action. It saddens me when looking at pastors' bookshelves to see how few have even one economics textbook or any serious ecological handbooks upon them; I have at least a shelf of each. Our lifestyles must reflect those brushstroke narratives which we must advocate daily.

Where to begin? Make some basic lifestyle changes—whether it is adopting an "Earth-friendly" diet (see below) or downsizing your home, heating needs, and expectations. Buy a couple of ecologically oriented-for-change books—whether on reducing your carbon footprint[2] or some big planetary answers[3]—and after passing them around friends, meet, eat, and talk about them. Then continue learning some more together.

Make dietary and lifestyle changes

One of the greatest differences we can make to our lives as globally responsible citizens is in reshaping our diet. This was the subject of my previous book, *What in God's Name are You Eating?*; borrow, beg, or buy a copy, but read it—please!

We can all reduce the amount of meat we eat, both portion and frequency. It takes 10 kg of plant material to produce 1 kg of meat; what else could be grown on the land needed for that 10 kg of vegetation? In contrast, 1 kg of insect protein requires only 1.7 kg of vegetable material to produce. Eat line-caught (or farmed) fish; trawling damages the ocean floor. As said above, eat more seasonal, locally produced vegetables while home-preserving or bottling local fruits and homegrown tomatoes, keeping a freezer for winter-only usage, to store harvested, inexpensive vegetable gluts. Join a Community Supported Agriculture scheme or productively work a community garden (UK=allotment), as we do, alongside raised

2. Berners-Lee, *How Bad are Bananas.*
3. Goodall, *Ten Technologies.*

vegetable beds, fruit trees, and a greenhouse in our backyard. Learn how to bake your own bread—even if only on weekends or your "day off"—it is inexpensive, helps heat your home, and is delicious. Do not waste anything—make compost.

The English phrase to "use your loaf" (i.e. head and brain) provides a useful mnemonic when food shopping. Buy:

L—local	locally produced meat, vegetables and fruit, in their own seasons;
O—organic	food produced without chemical pesticides and fuel-based fertilizers (e.g., baking your own bread with organic flour is cheaper than supermarket-bought bread);
A—animal friendly	humanely produced (and slaughtered) (e.g., "free-range" eggs, organic milk, refuse to buy meat from insensitively or crate-reared animals and birds, eat more wild-shot game);
F—"fair trade"	check on ethical and profit sharing with the original producers, for all tea, coffee, bananas/tropical fruits, recognizing the carbon footprint of all such imports.[4]

Commit to eating more locally produced foods. For example, in recent years we have grown to love quinoa but worried about buying even fair-trade versions because of the food miles involved. It is a great pseudocereal (i.e., similar to buckwheat), full of proteins, B vitamins, and dietary fibres, with vegetable leaves (to use like kale or spinach). Now we have found an English farmer who grows (literally) tons of quinoa here, harvesting it by machine; we have heard from Stateside friends of some North American farmers with a similar sandy-loam soil who can do the same. Even if locally grown quinoa is 20 percent more expensive, it is the price we must pay to help save the planet.

4. Berners-Lee, *How Bad are Bananas.*

Preserve habitats and species diversity

In Ireland, it is illegal to cut back hedges and grass verges between March and October, except for safety reasons. This then preserves these habitats for wild plants and flowers to germinate and seed, attracting bees and other insects and therefore birds; this maintains both plant and animal diversity. In Switzerland, car engines must be turned off at stop/red lights to help preserve local air quality.

Remember that Minnesotan trophy-hunting dentist. Species have to be allowed to find a natural numerical balance but that can be constrained by advancing human settlements (with attendant agriculture and livestock) and other human-led factors, such as pollution.

Outlaw unethical patterns of hunting—as Alaska has done in banning shooting of animals from boats and moving vehicles, including helicopters and light aircraft. There is no such thing as "canned hunting," it is organized killing when the prey species are somehow constrained, by bait, lack of space, tranquilization, or human socialization before being killed. Consider how South African "canned lion hunting" is damaging their wildlife tourist industry, which in 2016 employs one in seven of their population and creates R92bn of annual income.

"The best exercise of dominion now possible would be to make more space for other species to live their lives without human interference."[5] It may be necessary to have some globally monitored culling where habitats have become geographically restricted, to maintain natural balance so that neither alpha predators nor keystone herbivores destroy their own remaining habitats—while humankind restricts itself to increase that habitat. Consider what restraints now exist around Chernobyl (53–54) now that human banishment has effectively occurred.

Reduce consumption of everyday things

A mantra of the European and Australasian Green/eco-movement is "Reduce—Reuse—Recycle." How much stuff do we need? We can learn from backwoodsmen and homesteading communities, where little is thrown away and nearly everything is recycled (including building materials).

One of my simple pleasures when I first visited the USA was to be given one of those robust brown paper bags to carry my few purchases whether

5. Daly and Cobb, *For the Common Good*, 388.

I was in a grocery or liquor store or pharmacy. A small notice in a Ten Thousand Villages store (run by Mennonite friends) told me their brown bags are recycled paper. What a marked contrast with northern Europe and Australia, where flimsy plastic bags cause so much environmental damage, particularly to turtles and other marine creatures when they choke to death on them. In 2015, successive British and Australian reports showed that 90 percent of seabirds in the southern oceans had ingested plastic.

I was one of those who lobbied to restrict the issue of free plastic bags in the UK, encouraging forward legislation to charge (say US$15c) per bag issued. In Britain alone there has been a stunning reduction in the usage of such bags. Wales started charging in 2010 and has seen a 78 percent drop, while Northern Ireland began in 2013 causing a 71 percent drop there. In simple numerical terms, the drop is staggering: when charging began in Scotland in 2014, 147 million fewer bags were used—that is twenty-six bags per year for every man, woman, and child! England has now caught up; after similar charging began in 2015 in England, there was an 88 percent drop in use of plastic bags, during the first twelve months. If we consider that international environmental charities know that 8 million tons of nonbiodegradable plastics are washed up on our oceans' shorelines every year, we must do something. We need to stop using plastics, which are often energy-demanding oil or polymer based, for anything but absolute long-term needs; plastic disposables should be outlawed.

Change is needed and that will sometimes require the creation of prophetic legislation to force the populace to reduce consumption of environmentally harmful products—and not just plastics. How often do we need a new car? We as individuals, Christians, and church members need to be in the vanguard of working for that change, reducing consumption of increasingly scarce resources while reusing or recycling as much as we can. Do not use Styrofoam cups for coffee after worship.

"Teach your children well"

I love the Crosby, Stills, and Nash song entitled: "Teach Your Children"; look for it on your search engine and listen to it yourself.

Reduce your transport costs. Let your children go to school or college on the yellow bus, mass transport, or even long-distance Greyhound. Do you need Fed Ex to deliver everything? How many computers, TVs, laptops, and cell phones does your family home really *need*? If you're a Florida snowbird, is it better to fly south rather than take the RV? If Mom, Dad, or Grandma does things differently, so will our children!

Rethink your vacations! How often do you need to fly to Europe or coast to coast? My bucket list included driving Route 66, but my principles won't let me; anyone fancy car-sharing? Take the kids camping or hiking rather than long-distance touring. Using the "El" in Chicago or the underground in London may help cover big city distances, but check your map and sometimes walk—you can learn a lot more about the cities you visit. Discern the tourist attractions—choose quality wildlife attractions (with their accredited breeding groups), such as Bronx, San Diego, or Washington (USA), Chester (UK) or Taronga Park (Australia) zoos, rather than supporting the morally questionable captivity of orcas in SeaWorld (USA)[6] or Loro Parques (Europe) attractions.

Finally, have fewer children—let the earth breathe![7]

Technology helps . . .

I am a natural Luddite. I am slowly understanding the benefits of technology. I am writing this book on a relatively slow, four-year-old laptop that is still good to go. My bike's lights use rechargeable batteries.

Why does your employer insist you "take that trip" when Skype or conference calling is both more time and energy efficient? Technology has caught up with James Bond!

Think biblically

"Towards the end of the book of Ezekiel, the prophet is shown a vision of the land that once had been broken and turned to wilderness. But the bones of the dead have come back to life (Ezek. 37). The Earth, a new Eden, is restored by a stream that rises from the ground beneath a sacred place."[8] The biblical imagery of the restored place and the "river of life" encapsulates a trajectory from Genesis to Revelation.

While the pastor in me encourages the reading of the whole Bible, I am gradually understanding why we must teach *how* to read it to create

---

6. Kirby, *Death at Sea World.*

7. Emmott, *Ten Billion.*

8. McIntosh, *Soil and Soul,* 246.

greater daily encouragement, prayer, and activism. Begin with the Gospels' narratives of Jesus' life and teaching, then the diverse work on ministry in Acts; root that in the words and work of the Hebrew prophets, picking up on restored place/"river of life" passages before wrestling with the New Testament letters (which after all are answers to unwritten questions).

Make such biblical testimony live for you—heart, mind, and soul. Then make it an earthly reality in your daily life—generously in gift, gratitude, and language as well as lifestyle.

"Think global—campaign cooperatively—act local"

The slogan "Think global—campaign cooperatively—act local" has evolved through the international Green and eco-movements. Unwittingly, perhaps, it encapsulates biblical thinking, in calling everyone to adopt a thought-through world vision, which they are prepared to act upon at city, neighborhood, family, and individual levels. But that can only occur through "cooperative campaigning." This has two meanings: first, it is shared campaigning with others and not just those who share our ideology and, second, it means campaigning for the trajectory of that bigger vision, meaning that global citizens benefit and not just ourselves.

According to the US government, the risk of potential spillage and disastrous environmental damage to the Arctic is 75 percent. In the fortnight following Wimbledon's 2015 tennis tournament, tourists and office workers using the escalators at London's Waterloo underground station found many international celebrities, all wearing identical "Save the Arctic" T-shirts, staring back at them. Many of the office workers were from Shell's European headquarters nearby. There were already 7m global "Save the Arctic" supporters, as this London campaign was launched, encouraging more workers and tourists to join that campaign. During late fall 2015, Shell formally announced that the costs of such Arctic drilling were too high "on several fronts" and withdrew their proposals. This campaign worked!

The power of global campaigning for the environment and its future must continue.

Campaign—and donate to charities—wisely. More developing world deaths are due to poverty and disease than to natural disaster. Thus concerted campaigning and financial giving to charities that combat the underlying causes should be a priority but should not stop us giving further when there are disasters. My own support for the global charity Water Aid, documented elsewhere,[9] offers an example of this.

My radical Christian values include:

- Support for fair trade;

- Access to food, clean water, education, shelter, and health care for all;

- Justice for the world's people's and our fellow species;

- Believing in good research; sometimes we will be caught between "the lesser of two evils" (e.g., if child labor is *always* wrong, why do we let farmers' children work on their family farms or Native American children serve in their homeland shops? Is life in an Asian sweatshop preferable to subsistence existence in a flood-prone or drought-ridden village?); and

- Ensuring a healthy future for our planet and its diverse species.

You may add other things or phrase them differently. However, when I prayerfully consider these values, my reading of the Bible or daily "following after" Jesus, as well as the charities I financially support or campaign for and my everyday lifestyle, I can do no other than "think globally—campaign cooperatively—act locally."

9. Francis, *What in God's Name?*, 50

ECUMENY

7 "The Father and Mother of All Nations"

It was just another autumnal pastors' gathering for some Bible study, a shared meal, prayer ministry, and strategic planning. England's September rain meant some of us foregoing a wet walk to check the afternoon TV news, then watching in horror as the events of 9/11 unfolded in grim reality, before our powerless selves and in real time.

Some years later, I went with some fellow Princeton east-coasters to revisit the developing 9/11 memorial on the site of the former Twin Towers. We waited silently as some relatives of a few victims left their flowers and mementoes, listened to their pastor's wise prayer, and then turned away, mouthing, "Why?" Their inner feelings could not be vocalized. My doctoral colleagues found their own tears as they lost their voices, too. "You pray," one hoarsely whispered to me. It took the silent walk down through Battery Park and the round trip on the Staten Island ferry, passing Liberty's flame, to remind us that freedom has its price—and for our hearts, souls, and voices to recover some strength.

"Father *and* Mother"

The "and" in "Father and Mother" is important. What must be acknowledged is that in ancient civilizations, matriarchy or gender equality was just as likely as a patriarchal system. Archaeology and carbon dating show artifacts denoting female deities and/or earthly leaders from before Abrahamic times. The world's first named author was the female Sumerian poet Enheduanna, who was preserved as "the ice maiden" in Anatolia. Archaeological evidence from the nearby Eurasian steppes show a gender delineation in roles. Horse-riding men acted as itinerant warriors while women guarded the settlements as spiritual leaders and specialist tool workers (making harnesses and clothes) but with lethal weapons designed for a woman's smaller hand. All this makes sense, as childbearing women needed to be close to the home base, whereas warrior men are expendable, as a community's future only needs a few men for its progeniture, whereas it needs to safeguard *every* woman for childbearing. Polygamy might have become necessary.

Simultaneously, around 3000 BCE, further south in Assyria both polygamy and the veiling of women became known. Socially, this was precipitated by commodification, or women being regarded as the possessions of men, who kept their wives and daughters hidden in their homes. If the women wanted to go out, they would be veiled (effectively still hidden) and thus marked out from the bareheaded prostitutes and slave girls. Regrettably, this commodification of women, their resultant subjugation, and polygamy became normal behavior in the Middle East—the birthplace of the Abrahamic faiths.[1] Noting that men can be feminists, asserting the equal rights of women and men, we have to be aware of the innate patriarchalism and sexist language, as well as subjugating practices, of Abraham's faith and its successors.

Abrahamic faiths

Even atheists and secular commentators recognize the historical existence of the global numeric strength and the contemporary influence of the three present-day world faiths of Judaism, Christianity, and Islam. Some describe them as ethical monotheism; others as the Abrahamic faith or faiths. Together, the lives of these faiths are even more intertwined now than ever before—much of the fate of Planet Earth rests in their ongoing relationships and vision.[2]

Abram (or Abraham as he later became) is a central figure in the development of those three world faiths. In patriarchal society, sons were deemed vital to ensure one's line continued and to provide and protect in future days. Procreation was literally vital. So if sons did not occur with one's wife, one's concubine was used. The Genesis (11–25) narrative documents an occurrence of this.

1. Foreman, *World Made by Women*.
2. Peters, *Children of Abraham*.

To the Hebrew people, Abraham is *the* leading patriarch. How often do Jewish liturgy and prayers begin with the affirmation of the "God of Abraham, Isaac, and Jacob"? Note that Moses, the receiver of the Ten Commandments and leader of the exodus, is omitted from that select patriarchy. It was only when God told Abram, at the age of ninety-nine, that he was to be "the father of nations" (Gen 15:1–21) that God gave him the name Abraham and Sarai became Sarah; circumcision as a mark of God's blessing was also introduced in this same moment of declaration. Following years of barrenness, Abraham's wife Sarah conceived and bore him a son, Isaac. This precious son was famously dragged into the wilderness as a boy by his father, who believed that God wanted him to sacrifice this son and future of God's people. God stayed Abraham's hand in favor of a thicket-caught ram and the rest became history as the campfire story was handed through generations into written Scripture.[3] But with Isaac's birth, Abraham set aside his firstborn son, Ishmael, and his mother, Hagar, a concubine.

For Christians, Abraham is both a historic figure and a leading patriarch in Israel's past. However, Christian belief focuses around the earthly person of Jesus of Nazareth as both its key figure and human exemplar. Whatever my Westernized education tells me, against its background of postwar British chauvinism, Jesus' attitude to women is one that I find exhilarating and enjoyably challenging. Jesus' New Testament encounters with Mary his mother, Mary Magdalene, the Syro-Phoenician woman, the woman in the crowd who touched him, or the one who is about to be stoned, or Mary and Martha challenge every preconception that UK society (but not my parents) wanted me to espouse.

Although Jesus is central to our understandings of God's intentions, it is the new community, which he is calling into being, that provides supportive examples of how we live as disciples.[4] Christian faith is just as much about mothering and nurture as it is a demand from a patriarchal father. That is somewhat emphasized by the fact that there are only twenty-two New Testament verse references to Abraham. Nearly half of these refer to a Judaic concept of Abraham's heritage; most are quoted by epistle writers, and only two are placed on the lips of Jesus (Matt 8:11; John 8:56). Christianity is a Jesus-shaped egalitarian discipleship rather than an Abrahamic-patterned domination.

3. Fretheim, *Abraham*.
4. Francis, *Shalom*.

Islam, which means "submission" in Arabic, was founded in AD 632 when the last of their lawful prophets, Muhammad, died, having received the Qu'ran—God's sacred gift to the world, which demands human response and worship. Just like the Presbyterian Westminster Confession, which proclaims that "the chief end of *man* is to glorify [worship] God," Islam is similarly unequivocal in asserting that such worship transcends every aspect of life, and so must include fivefold daily prayer or *salat*. The Qu'ran has several references to preceding lawful prophets—Adam, Noah, Abraham, Moses, and Jesus, as in the Bible—as well as Mary, honoring them all as holy people. The Qu'ran is divided into 114 *suras*, or chapters, which break down into over 6,300 verses.[5] I do not read Arabic so cannot understand the nuancing that caused Islam to have three major factions—Sunni, Shi'ite, and Sufi; each has its own forms and practices of radicality and behavior.[6]

However, Ishmael is a renowned prophet throughout Islam. The Qu'ran acknowledges him as the firstborn of Abraham (Ibrahim), by Hagar (the concubine who was Sarai's servant). Although the Qu'ran is unclear, Islam believes that Abraham was going to sacrifice Ishmael, not Isaac, before God/Allah provided a ram instead. Contrary to the biblical narrative, the Qu'ran makes clear that Abraham took Hagar and Ishmael to Mecca, where later Ishmael was responsible for it becoming the destination of Islamic pilgrimage—or *hajj*.[7] The Qu'ran sets forward the five core practices of Islam: the *shahadah*, or confession that Allah is the only God, *salat*, or daily prayer, *zakat*, or almsgiving (which can be money, food, clothes, or shelter), *sawmi*, or fasting at prescribed times and festivals, and the *hajj*, at least once in every Moslem's lifetime. In the exposition and interpretation of these practices, Ibrahim the prophet is declared to have undertaken them all.

The history of the world for more than 1,300 years has been defined by the struggles, interfaith violence, and relationships between these three Abrahamic faiths. The agendas created as each began continues through 9/11 and is with us into the long-term future. What does that mean?

5. Pickthall, *Meaning of the Glorious Koran.*
6. Armstrong, *Islam.*
7. Parfitt and Nini, eds., *Israel and Ishmael.*

Christendom and the Caliphate

For nearly three centuries after Jesus' resurrection, Christianity existed and grew as a countercultural movement. The New Testament bears witness to household communities of faith and increasing gender equality in church leadership. Literature from the Romans and others of their contemporaries tells of the violent persecution of Christians—think lions. Catacombs throughout the Mediterranean have art, however crude, portraying this. Christianity grew out from the Levant through household communities, itinerant evangelism, and the witness of coenobitic monasticism.[8] Certainly, some scholarship insists that Christianity traveled west into Celtic lands[9] and at least as far as India[10] to the east.

Politically, in the fourth century everything changed. Following Constantine's conversion, it was the Roman Emperor Theodosius who established Christianity as the *official* religion of the empire by outlawing other religions, by a series of laws beginning from 381 onwards.[11] Assent to formalized creeds (orthodoxy) and practices became the test of faith rather than Jesus-shaped discipleship (orthopraxy). Christendom was thus established.[12]

Whether it was Catholicism in the Mediterranean countries, Lutheranism in the Germanic and Nordic nations or Anglicanism in England, Holy Mother Church became a key establishment player across Europe. Those who dissented were persecuted by church and state alike, which resulted in the Crusades, the Spanish Inquisition, and the burning or beheading of martyrs in Tudor England and mainland Europe. Disestablishment and moribund denominationalism are gradually sweeping Europe in

---

8. Coenobitic monasticism differs immensely from later or classical monasticism, which involved monks living in close community within a complex of buildings, including dormitories, refectories, and a large church, often boundaried by high walls (such as late-medieval Benedictine or Cistercian houses). In marked contrast, coenobites were predominantly hermits who lived out a threefold rule (prayer, work, and renunciation) who only gathered together on Sundays or major holy days, often in a cave or forest glade but rarely a communal building. Coenobitism was typified by the second century Desert Fathers or the early Celtic monastic settlements.

9. Bowen, *Saints, Seaways and Settlements.*

10. Fernando and Sauch-Gispert, *Christianity in India.*

11. Kreider, *Patient Ferment of the Early Church.*

12. Kreider, *Origin of Christendom.*

a post-Christendom tide, while in marked contrast their former colonial mission churches continue to grow.[13]

Economically, Christendom established hierarchies, allowing bishops to wear the imperial purple, and economic systems of suppression, including tithes and other church (33–34). In my lifetime, older hymnals often contained the verse of the hymn "All Things Bright and Beautiful" by Cecil Francis Alexander in 1848:

The rich man in his castle,

The poor man at his gate,

God made them, high or lowly,

And ordered their estate.

When I went to seminary, one advocated key text was Max Weber's *The Protestant Work Ethic and the Spirit of Capitalism* to help us "understand the world's order."[14] How wrong we were to blindly assume that establishment Protestantism should support capitalist endeavor when it really should be proclaiming the egalitarian "reign of God" as defined by Jesus of Nazareth. No wonder people increasingly reject the institutional church because it has tied itself to such a flawed political and economic system, which Christendom helped create.

For nearly three centuries, following Muhammad the Prophet's death in 632, Islam underwent both expansion and a "golden age." It was an age of medical and scientific discovery.[15] Doctors were licensed and what we can recognize as hospitals opened, offering far more than the palliative or hospice care of the infirmaries of classical western (Christian) monasticism. Islamic scholars invented algebra (*al-jibbar*) and used the same data as Copernicus used, nearly a millennium later, to posit heliocentrism. It was an age of culture, as Islamic nonfigurative art became common[16] and writers such as the Persian poet, Rumi, became known and widely read.[17] It coincided with the founding of a small Andalusian citadel which over the next five centuries became the Alhambra Palace—still an architectural jewel.

13. Murray, *Post-Christendom.*

14. Weber, *Protestant Ethic.*

15. Masood, *Science and Islam.*

16. Rice, *Islamic Art.*

17. Jamal, *Islamic Mystical Poetry.*

Politically, all this wonderment coincided with the infighting between different factional heads over who, with their sons, should become the right dynastic leaders to succeed "the Prophet." To keep the nations united to single Islamic purpose, the concept of a caliphate developed. While each nation would retain their own leaders, kings, or princes, there would be an overarching empire of all these countries, presided over and led by a single caliph (*khalif*), hence caliphate. It would need a return to a form of fundamentalist understanding of the Qu'ran, as revealed by Muhammad the Prophet, to ensure the caliphate could move together as one entity. That would require an acceptance of hierarchy, religious observance, and suppression of those offering an alternative worldview. This is why contemporary Islamist extremists *may* be portrayed as Islamic fundamentalists, who advocate a global caliphate and the violent extermination of those who oppose that purpose.[18] "Apart from Western misunderstanding of Islam as a politically-friendly religion, we have the additional problem of misunderstanding the Muslim transformation of the secular state, a transformation in which the state acquires moral infallibility by becoming a funnel of the norms of *Shari'ah*."[19]

Economically, there is a diversity of wealth among Muslims—think Saudi Arabia or the Bin Laden building companies. As in Jewish law, the Qu'ran forbids usury, and any other lending of money for profit, so that Muslims use forms of sharia mortgages or credit associations for business and housing purchase or development. Apart from the Gulf States, generally there is an Islamic rejection of personal ostentation or wealth display, and many societies have an egalitarian approach in clothing, housing, and lifestyle, appropriate to their geographical locus. I recall our Bengali waiter excusing himself from our table-side conversation in a downtown restaurant in Birmingham, UK, to make his weekly without-interest payment of his house loan to an "uncle" walking by; there was no embarrassment for any of us. Such a different economic approach emphasizes why some want a caliphate to establish a new world order distinct from Westernized, allegedly Christian, economics.

18. Armstrong, *Battle for God*.
19. Newbigin, Sanneh, and Taylor, *Faith and Power*, 28.

Jihad and God's world empires

By the time of 9/11, Western media often used the phrase "McWorld" to describe consumerist countries, which were also consumed by their own upward economic growth. No wonder the targets of 9/11 and the Pentagon were seen as representing bastions of economic and military power.

US citizens need no reminder that 9/11 was the first "homeland" assault since Pearl Harbour in 1941. In both attacks, there was a clash of empires. For reasons outlined earlier in this book, the USA had deliberately set out to become the leader of the "free world." Postwar, it had used its monetary policies to control the economic redevelopment of northern hemisphere, Westernized nations. It had also used its military might and technology to act as the "world's policeman," creating an unusual security for those who played by the USA's rules. In Europe this became known as *Pax Americana*, because of its similarity in style to the *Pax Romana* of 2,000 years before. A nation whose currency says "In God We Trust," and whose president ends virtually every speech with "God bless America" is, deliberately or not, claiming that it is a blessed and holy nation.

It is little wonder that Allah-fearing Muslims, who follow the Qu'ran inerrantly view the supposedly Christianized west and particularly America's alleged decadence as requiring both verbal denunciation and physical attack. The clash becomes a "holy war" between ideological worldviews within the Abrahamic faiths. Often the Arabic word *jihad* is applied to that clash, but its literal meaning is "struggle," in the sense of actively striving by as many Qu'ran-permitted means as possible to retain the purity of Islam.

After 9/11 Benjamin Barber, the Rutgers professor of political science, revised his influential *Jihad v. McWorld*.[20] His thesis can be summarized in two quotes: "The dynamics of the Jihad-McWorld linkage is deeply dialectical"[21] and "more recently, Jihad has been both fostered and contradicted by McWorld's postmodernity."[22] His analysis is important because it not only demonstrates how the tensions between Islam and the Christianized West are fostered by their interface and seemingly different attitudes to consumerism but also highlights how transnational economics wield forces that threaten even the global Abrahamic faiths. But there is a significant danger in the Westernized-style analysis of Barber (and many others): it

20. Barber, *Jihad v. McWorld*.
21. Ibid., 18.
22. Ibid., 161.

creates a confrontational polarity between Islam and the West's Christianity. We need to recover a more helpful mutual starting point in the Qu'ran's teaching (3:64), which addresses both Jews and Christians as "People of the Book," acknowledging that we share a common purpose because we all worship the same God.

The failure of the Enlightenment

The Enlightenment, is also known as the Age of Reason, ran from the 1620s to the 1780s through all the European nations from Russia westwards. It drew together philosophical, cultural, scientific, and intellectual forces, arguing that reason and analysis, as well as individualism, should predominate—rather than the traditional lines of authority, such as the Christendom church.

There had been several recent centuries of retrenchment and even Islamic nominalism, so much so that during the Enlightenment, it was the rise of secularism that became the Christendom Church's conversation partner rather than another faith.[23] To generalize, the church rejected any concept of alternative forms of authority, whether (among many examples) it was Galileo's heliocentrism and Isaac Newton's scientific theorems or Descartes's and Voltaire's assertions that a secular philosophy could actually exist. A key failure of the Enlightenment was its inability to create dialogue or conversation between those holding differing worldviews.[24]

This lack of interface with an increasingly secular worldview, now represented by scientism and/or humanism, is but one of the fears of the fundamentalist Islamic State "organization." Hence their wholesale antagonism to Westernized lifestyle values. It is not so long since the Christian West was practicing genocide and persecution, as well as burning or beheading apostate believers; so our contemporary criticisms need to be tempered by our own murderous history. A key issue in this is a particular religion's (or a faction of it) understanding of the inerrancy of its own Scripture, be that the Talmud, the Bible, or the Qu'ran.

After the US Supreme Court ruled in 2015 that same-sex marriages were legal, the jailing of the Rowan County, Kentucky, county clerk for "contempt of court" in refusing to issue such marriage licenses made international headlines. She claimed this was because her Christian faith, with

23. Akhtar, *Light in the Enlightenment.*
24. Cragg, *Church in an Age of Reason.*

its inerrant view of Scripture, did not sanction same-sex relationships or marriages. Jesus reminded his followers to deal "with the log in their own eyes, before the splinters in others' eyes" (Luke 6:42); therefore the church has a lot of internal work to do before criticizing those who take inerrant views of the Torah or Qu'ran.

Another failure of the Enlightenment, with its propositional view of advancing argument, is that the church did not absorb the lesson that theology (our understanding of God and the world) can progress creatively if we adopt such a propositional style of argument and counterargument. Failure to recognize the validity of other views leads to restrictions upon everyone's freedom (religious and other) and creates suspicion of anyone who holds to other patterns of thought.[25]

Freedom, suspicions, and religious (in)tolerance

Freedom of faith and freedom to believe are precious—as is the right to practice those freedoms without threat or violence from others, assuming that such practice is also nonviolent and peacemaking. Statute and just law enforcement rather than vigilante retribution need to be the corrective for those whose faith or belief causes harm. Problematically, when someone identified with a particular faith's stance speaks out in favour of tolerance or even reconciliation, they are treated with suspicion. I recall the furor from the traditional Orthodox Jewish community when in 2002, the UK's then-Chief Rabbi Jonathan Sacks published *The Dignity of Difference*, with its overarching plea and gracious advocacy for religious tolerance.

We live in a world of deep suspicions. As this decade unfolds, it is easy to understand some British xenophobia towards the fact that Chinese funding is being used to control and build French-leased nuclear power plants on either side of southern England. What is the controlling worldview in all this—secular, profiteering economics or ecology? Likewise, when the US Environmental Protection Agency in 1998 found both Ford and Honda "guilty" of using software to dupe emission tests, rumors circulated in the car industry that the practice was becoming more sophisticated and widespread. Enter Volkswagon-Audi's recent self-admitted similar software usage and we can justly ask questions about candor and motive, when such duplicitous economic pursuit overrides all moral, Abrahamic-ethic, and ecological considerations.

25. Pearse, *Age of Reason*.

From fiction such as Graham Greene's *The Third Man*, through contemporary award-winning TV series (like the US's *Homeland* or the UK's *Spooks*), we live in a world of nations, predicated upon suspicions, espionage, and often preemptive violence. One only needs to read Peter Wright's *Spycatcher* or Frederick Forsyth's *The Outsider* to discover how international espionage works, often violently and preemptively, to engender public suspicions and xenophobia (particularly within Westernized nations). Both these writers were warned by their spymasters not to publish and the UK government spectacularly failed through the courts to suppress Wright.

However, we do need to be cautious about what is put in the public domain, and those of us who write must review potential consequences before publication. Many readers will remember the furor (and consequent *fatwa*) about Salman Rushdie's 1988 novel, *The Satanic Verses*, that begins with two Islamic figures falling to earth from the plane which one of them had just exploded in the skies. Just over a year later, a PanAm flight was bombed out of the UK skies by Libyans, as their leader Gaddafi later admitted. In 2002, Michel Houllebecq's novel *Platform* was centered around the beach shooting of western tourists by Islamist terrorists; in 2015, something similar occurred in Tunisia. Khaled Hosseini's novel *A Thousand Splendid Suns* tells of the tragic suppression of women within extremist Islam—easily synonymous with caliphate advocacy. There are fine lines between descriptive fiction, creating xenophobia, and offering strategies to the "trigger happy."

It is easy to create religious hatred but so complex to peaceably heal the divisions created. For many years, Christians lived with an intrinsic anti-Semitism because they perceived that the Jews were *entirely* responsible for Jesus' crucifixion. The complicity of both Lutheran and Roman Catholic authorities with such views allowed the Nazis to proceed, almost without criticism, with their pogroms and the Holocaust. To create fear and antagonism towards others of a different color or those who peacefully practice a different (to our own) faith is morally wrong. It certainly conflicts with the peacemaking Jesus of Nazareth's views and leads to racial and religious division. Those who witnessed 9/11 should reflect upon how much Islamophobia we have witnessed since then—and ask ourselves, how often have we objected to such attitudes?

As Jesus tells us, we must look at the logs in our own eyes before pointing out the splinters in those of others. How much has our western, sometimes Christianized, history demonized all of Islam because of the actions of a few murderous fanatics?[26] How much would Christians want their whole faith to be judged only by the actions of the twelfth-century Crusades or the later Spanish Inquisition?

I was not born in 1948 when Westernized nations colluded to forge the State of Israel. There was a sense of "at last, a precious homeland for God's Hebrew people." I enjoy visiting Israel, with its varied cities and countryside, have relished eating food produced locally with few "food miles" and rejoiced in my welcome in *kibbutzim* (7). But I do question how some of that Jewish nation, who have suffered through millennia, *and* forced expulsions, *and* the Holocaust, want now to become violent oppressors. I thank God that Prime Minister Netanyahu has repeatedly and unequivocally condemned those "extremist Jewish people" who have attacked and burned out Palestinian settlers. It will take more than a few stones and a slingshot to rescue the Israelites if the Goliath of the Palestinians' Arab neighbors raise their hand against Israel (1 Sam 17).

Jesus was decisive in dealing with those who sought to mete out "rough justice," particularly when they used religious pretexts for doing it. When he invited those about to stone the woman caught in adultery, with "Let whoever is without sin cast the first stone" (John 8:7), the crowd melted away. The Jews in first-century Galilee were xenophobic about Arabs. No wonder Jesus told a parable about a good Samaritan (Jesus never said he was "the" or the only good Samaritan), and was prepared to sit with the woman at the well in Samaria (John 4), much to the concern of the Twelve, as Samaria and its people were Arab. To some contemporary Western eyes, Arab nations are viewed as automatically Muslim and worse, to our shame, some of those watchers see all such people as terrorists. Churches, synagogues, and mosques need to promote interfaith learning about peace and justice issues so that suspicions can be diminished, tolerance is renewed,[27] and freedom of faith is honored.

But as Geert Mak, that eminent Dutch social philosopher points out:

> Unrest has grown among Europe's seventeen million Muslims. Are we still welcome? Do we still belong? In this way, in recent years, Europe has become the unwilling front-line in a conflict that ultimately must be fought out within Islam itself, a conflict concerning how such a traditional world religion must deal with

---

26. Sardar and Davies, *Distorted Imagination*, 76–87.

27. Clark, *Abraham's Children*.

secularisation, globalisation, individual liberties, women's rights,
and all the rest that goes with a modern society.[28]

While Mak is correct, Christians ought to remember Jesus' words about logs
and splinters before confronting others about their support for Qu'ranic or
Talmudic attitudes.

Those who struggle with this need to recognize my rooting in the
demonstrably peacemaking Anabaptist Christian tradition, which calls for
interfaith dialogue for exactly the reasons outlined in my previous para-
graphs. But this peacemaking tradition is not alone either within contemporary Christianity (e.g., Christ-centered Quakers) or reforming Judaism
(cf. Jonathan Sacks's 2015 book: *Not in God's Name: Confronting Religious
Violence*).

Ergo . . .

If Abraham is seen as a patriarch or father figure within the three world
ethical and monotheistic faiths, then those who peacefully nurture such
beliefs and behavior act like their mother "just as a hen gathers her chicks"
(Luke 13:34). Whether that is bishops and pastors, rabbis, or imams, or the
"communities of faith" that gather in churches, synagogues, and mosques
respectively is not irrelevant, but it is the teaching and service to neigh-
bor that emerges from them, which helps to define their understanding of
nationhood.

Each of these global Abrahamic faiths has separate understandings
about what such nationhood should mean, whether it has been Christendom, "the land of Israel," or the caliphate. The challenge in today's world
is how they *must* learn peacefully to coexist, and as they are challenged
necessarily to do so by secularists, scientism, and other world faiths such as
Buddhism, Hinduism, and Sikhism.

Abraham symbolizes humanity in his desire to fulfill God's big intention for the world around him. Like all of us, Abraham *may* be criticized for
missing some God's lesser intentions—was the setting aside of Hagar and
Ishmael part of God's intention, too? There is hardly a world nation which
does not have communities of one or more of the Abrahamic faiths, whose
witness and service affects not just their immediate neighborhood but also
the nature of that nation itself. Abrahamic faith does act as the father and

28. Mak, *In Europe*, 813.

mother of nations. The question is how we can overcome historic enmities and became one people, working together for the good of this one God-given world. Time for another chapter?

8 "That they may be one"

When the Harvard professor of public policy becomes a household name because several US presidents seek his counsel, you know something is going on. That man is Robert Putnam. His thesis is simple: American society is fragmenting. No longer are people joining clubs, churches, and political parties; despite what the pundits would have you believe, the membership of all these organizations is falling. From the moment the quasi-fictional Joad family arrived in California to be bullied by resettlement officials, the writing was on the wall.[1] America was breaking up into an even more class-ridden society. Such a society had existed since the days of slaves and masters, as enshrined in the Declaration of Independence.

Fragmentation

Gated communities are just as much part of the US middle class, from Florida to Oregon, as they once were for the rich, wealthy, and sometimes famous, whether along Westchester Avenue, New York, or the Hollywood canyons of California. Even black, Hispanic, and white racial groups are stratifying. One only needs to witness a presidential campaign to know how important media-covered rallies for "urban Hispanics" or "rural poor whites" or "black college students" have become. Is the land of the free still the home of the brave, and can they stand as one under that star-spangled banner?[2]

1. Steinbeck, *Grapes of Wrath.*
2. Putnam, *Bowling Alone*; Putnam, *Our Kids.*

To be fair, the USA has always had a stratified society, which popular pundits and sociologists have defined in a number of ways, dividing rich and poor, haves and have-nots, celebrity or undesirable, and for many years as black or white. What changed this was the huge advance in both consumerism and advertising from the 1950s, through the Vietnam era to the present day. It is commonly understood that average wages in the USA rose by 80 percent between 1947 and 1970, just as advertising, television, and the ubiquity of consumer goods occurred. This also the coincided with the postwar explosion in catalogue shopping, enabling even the poor to have goods *now* while paying a lot of interest as well as the capital cost over many future weeks—"the never-never." In its turn that paved the way for an addiction to debt with the growing ubiquity of credit (cards).

Learning from others

Not all the history of Western nations' colonies has been so economically driven. The contemporary nations of Kenya, Uganda, and Tanzania—all former European colonies—are transforming themselves into mixed economy nations, supporting subsistence farming, itinerant herding, and wildlife eco-tourism while seriously questioning dependence upon Westernized monocultural agriculture and urbanizing development. Their indigenous regionalization saw these three nations form a trading confederation in 2001: the East African Community, which celebrated an equality of partnership between them.

Former French Indo-China is made up of proud independent (once again) nations. In AD 41 in Vietnam, the leadership of two warrior women, the Trung sisters, ousted their Chinese colonizers. Their reforms of an egalitarian (gender included) agrarian-based village confederation were violently destroyed within two years by the reinvading Han dynasty army. China reinstated their patriarchal, Confucian-based, growth-oriented, trading society for the next 900 years. A millennium later, after the uneasy French occupation, Ho Chi Minh and the Viet Cong reinstituted the Trung sisters' systems of land reform and decentralized village democracy,[3] only to be halted for a decade by napalm and the American offensive of the Vietnam War.[4]

3. Lien and Sharrock, *Descending Dragon.*
4. Karnow, *Vietnam.*

Without becoming stridently feminist, it is relatively easy to see the Confucian corruption of the I Ching upon Chinese society, two millennia ago. Although the I Ching insisted upon harmonious and equal complementarity of Yin-Yang, such as darkness and light, female and male, Confucianism demanded patriarchy and the subjugation of Yin/women. Not even the Chinese Cultural Revolution from 1949 onward restored the equality of women; a pattern still noted in parts of contemporary Chinese society. The lesson here is that however egalitarian any philosophy is, it requires the whole society to both intuitively then actively work to maintain such complementary values—or else society fragments. Gender inequality is a major failure of a world to be "as one." Fragmentation is everywhere.

For Europeans, this is evident. In the north, the strained relations between Russia and other former Soviet republics, especially Ukraine, are evident in the violent confrontations each has with Russia. The partitioning of Ireland and the divisions between Catholic and Protestant communities still requires much healing; I work on this chapter during the centennial commemoration of the 1916 Easter Rising. Following the breakup of Yugoslavia, past religious and racial enmities erupted into the murderous Balkan wars. The Scottish Referendum in 2014 produced 45 percent in favor of independence, while Spain's regional elections in 2015 reaped a majority Catalonian assembly in favour of Basque separatism. At the Celtic fringes, Cornish and Breton (France) separatists take heart and ideas from the Manx Parliament and the Welsh Assembly. When does fragmentation become blind nationalism, rather than a step towards complementary statehood for the common good of all? "Christian citizens should challenge the idolatry of an exclusive national identity."[5]

Jesus said, and taught by example, that his disciples should be "as one" (John 17:21). Whether it is the ubiquity of television, the Internet, and attendant technology or the global market, we are being lulled by transnational companies and "growth economics" towards a false vision of "one world." For everything that seems to help us take a step forward also brings often unseen, larger negative factors that destroy such unity. Christians and all communities of faith must learn how to question, then diminish those negatives without resorting to the violence of colonial warfare or Islamic State extremism. This chapter seeks to review some of these major issues, which affect the unity of all God's people.

5. Friesen, *Artists, Citizens, Philosophers*, 249.

The global market

In my teens, I met a Kenyan student whose first name was Kelloggs because his parents had liked the name they saw on a billboard. Advertising is transforming global culture. I have drunk Coca-Cola in Russia and even sat in McDonalds in Indonesia. The global market has arrived—but the world is fragmenting.

North America is a consumerist continent, taking up far more of Earth's resources than is biblically or morally just for that small percentage of the global population. What must be recognized is whether 28 or 35 percent (dependent upon who is counting) of global resources should be consumed by that 5 percent of the world's population in the USA and Canada. This is a global injustice.

I used to think commercialism and consumerism were bad in Britain. That became even more apparent after living in rural southwest France. Driving down to Bordeaux airport to meet friends and family, I was aware how quickly I was approaching France's sixth largest conurbation as the billboards and cheap motels lined the approach roads, and branded stores crowded the *autoroute* (freeway) junctions. That was such a marked contrast to the clean uncluttered approaches to Scandinavian cities. Britain seemed in overload on my return, then I went back to the USA . . . .

I now understand more of the brilliance of the pop art movement, in utilizing everyday billboard commercialism, repeating images of products and celebrity faces (Warhol), the deep black lines of the comic-book–styled lives (Bolshier and Lichtenstein) or giant-size sculptures of insignificant daily objects (Oldenberg and Van Bruggen). Warhol's "soup can art" then or the contemporary Chinese artist who has now set up a supermarket simply selling the whole range of (empty) packaging challenge the nature of the consumerist boom.[6]

What the Pop Art Movement foretold in the 1950s and 1960s was that everything is going to be commodified, even people; "everybody will have their fifteen minutes of fame" as the multiplying forms of reality TV demonstrate. Recently I heard a Florida tourist express preference for the animatronic models at a theme park "because there they do not smell like the real animals." D'oh! Every experience or commodity can have its seeming market value but this does not truly reflect *and include* its environmental costs.

6. Lippard, *Pop Art*.

Is everything in the balance?

The upside of a global market, whether of commodities or experiences, is that those with the resources buy whatever they want from wherever they want. The innate danger within that is the unseasonal and unreasonable use of raw materials by an unbalanced percentage of the world's population. This has huge ecological consequences. But "The practical consequence is that people can no longer grow their beans and their grains. Their subsistence is no longer secured by the world trade model of the free market. Our economic order is an order of exploitation which produces hunger and destruction."[7] Those at the bottom of the world's heap are being denied even their subsistence lives because of Westernized demands.

Just after the turn of the millennium, East Africa discovered that abandoning subsistence farming in favor of revenue-producing monocropping for European markets has ecological consequences for its populace, native species, and the land. The great American dustbowl of the 1930s and 1940s is a previous example of consumerism creating bad ecology, consigning the poor to the wrong side of the line.

Two further downsides of a global market are that the rich think they live in a 1960s world when they believe they can travel wherever they want, without paying the true planetary cost. Currently 80 percent of all the world's goods are moved by international shipping. The fact that ship transit is the world's third biggest polluter after the USA and China tells us that financially everything must cost more if environmentally balancing/reparative costs are to be factored in, for the common good.

Politically, the interdependence of the global market has to be increasingly (if not immediately) counterbalanced by the fact that "ecological economics" are properly factored in by both transnationals and government levy or taxation. The equation "one world=one market" means that individuals, nations, and shareholders will have to pay more and accept less.

Migrants and refugees

In a world of developing interfaith/geopolitical tensions as well as a rising global population, it is unsurprising there will be more migrants and refugees. How the world and its constituent nations treats such people,

7. Soelle, *Thinking about God*, 90–91.

particularly those described as "displaced" because of those tensions, becomes a vital question of uniting global responsibility.

For the preaching, prayers, and pastoral reflection of every ecumenically committed, outward-looking congregation, to dwell upon the Christian, moral, and political obligation to care for the "widow, orphan, and stranger" (Deut 10:18; 27:19) helps us truly recognize them as our sisters and brothers in need—and not as scroungers or an alien species. The church has real ecumenical responsibility to ensure that the "flight into Egypt" (Matt 2:13–23) forms at least a biennial focus of the annual lectionary. This would enable the narrative of Jesus, Mary, and Joseph's self-exile from violent tyranny in north Africa to help Christians worshipfully reflect upon our shared response to migrants and refugees.

Border controls may *seem* a political (and even economic) necessity, but they have to be morally permeable. We cannot shut our doors, boundaries, and hearts to those in need. Arguments can be formed for maintaining strong US border controls, providing that Mexicans and Canadians as well as those arriving at airports all receive exactly equal treatment. No one who remembers the Black Power salute on the Olympic podium in 1968 should forget the second-placed white Australian expressing his solidarity against the "white Australia policy." Border controls are intrinsically divisive, requiring constant review against injustice. This was one reason why the European Union effectively created a borderless state at Schengen from 1995; only Britain and Ireland chose the then legally allowed opt-out.

The EU believed such "freedom of movement" would not allow repetition of the great migrant crisis, following the Second World War, when millions of citizens were displaced, often becoming stateless. However, it has been the various nations' churches acting ecumenically that have helped politicians and legislators to understand that "freedom of movement" does not have to presume "rights to citizenship" nor "health care tourism" but does demand proper welcome, health care, and registration for all migrants, refugees, and displaced persons.

We can learn from the informal solo courage of Frère Roger's "welcome" in war-torn, poverty-stricken Taizé through to the concerted response of Greek Orthodox congregations now that we must act prophetically in meeting the needs of refugees and migrants—the "strangers" in Hebrew scripture.

A changing world

However, the violence of various Islamic State militants has precipitated another great migrant and refugee crisis. In the five years since 2010, the population of Lebanon had increased by 25 percent. That is one refugee for every four citizens—now imagine that in your town or country. In 2013, Syria had 23 million people; because of in-country violence; by 2015, half of Syria's population had become displaced persons living elsewhere, mainly in Lebanon or northern Europe. The failure of the global community, particularly larger Arab/Muslim states, to heal the weeping sores of the Syrian and other regional conflicts is causing mayhem.

The EU's Schengen Agreement is failing because of the vast number of refugees arriving daily, as some Greek islands report they "are receiving another ten thousand migrants every day." It is frightening and challenging to realize how much the churches in Britain, France, Germany, the Netherlands, and Scandinavia must live prophetically, calling their own governments to account while offering *our own* spare bedrooms to house such refugees. The agenda created by both the Middle Eastern wars and consequent European migrant crisis will be continuing long after this book is published. In 2014, 250,000 migrants arrived in Europe, in 2015 that figure doubled, and as this book's text goes to my editor in 2016, that annual figure has risen again.

One of our respected colleagues in the UK's missional debate has written: "The next decades will surely be marked by increasing vulnerability and insecurity for humanity and this will have profound effects not only on the comforts we have been used to, but will inevitably lead to sharper polarisations in many aspects of economic, social and environmental justice."[8] When in June 2016, the UNHCR says that currently there are sixty-five million migrant-refugees in the world, such Christian concern is well founded.

Population, health, lifestyle, and diet

There can be little argument with either United Nations statistics or World Health Organization figures that our planet has a rising population, which in the long term must be reversed, and presently must adapt to meet the needs of all and not just a privileged few—normally Westerners.

8. Kingston-Smith, "Migrants, Justice and Border Lives," 102.

Health care impacts every individual and family. I would not be alive to write now had it not been for top-quality UK cardiac surgery, care, and daily medication during the past decade. Whatever your moral thinking, my partner and wider family believe that to be money well spent, even if its total cost has been equal to or more than my lifetime's taxation. But what is done is done and I draw the line at further intervention, refusing to enter discussion about whether I should be on the transplant list. Of course not; the 35-year-old parent, with young children, chronic cardiomyopathy, and their life still ahead of them is far more morally deserving of a transplant than I who have "had a life," seen the world, written books, loved, and been loved.

The economics of Westernized health care is exponentially rising. This is not the book to explore the morality of self-administered voluntary euthanasia but the example of Oregon, the Netherlands, or Switzerland must provide a voice into that discussion. We all have to know when "enough is enough," receiving palliative care and pain relief rather than prolonging expensive treatment. This is a debate that the church has to enter prophetically and conducting proper research, even potentially initiating it.

Health care economics

In spring 2016, the World Health Organization published figures showing that in 1980 there were 108 million cases of diabetes but that it had quadrupled to 422 million by 2014. Figures revealed that between 2005 and 2015, the incidence of UK diabetes rose by 60 percent to 3.3 million people (5 percent of the population!). The cost of treatment and medication was US$16bn/£10bn or 10 percent of the UK's National Health Service allocated revenue budget.

Frustratingly, the quoted WHO statistics did not differentiate between Type 1 and Type 2 diabetes. Type 1 diabetes is genetically determined (appearing to remain static percentage-wise within each ethnic population), whereas Type 2 diabetes is lifestyle-related, caused by a poor, sugar-rich diet, lack of exercise, etc. Ninety percent of UK diabetics have Type 2, and the cost of their medication and the consequent treatments for blindness, heart disease, and amputations could have been avoided—if those individuals had changed their lifestyles.[9]

9. Francis, *What in God's Name?*, 79-80.

Frighteningly, World Health Organization projections indicate that the USA's incidence of Type 2 diabetes will be between two and four times percentage-wise that of the UK by 2030. The cost and social implications are horrendous. Trusted friends who have researched diabetes incidence in both the Netherlands and Scandinavia have discovered little evidence to show any significant rise in Type 2 diabetes in those countries, suggesting they are either better educated to avoid its arrival or the population is living a healthier lifestyle. In Australasia, the incidence of lifestyle-related heart disease, strokes, obesity, and Type 2 diabetes are several percentage points of population below those of their northern hemisphere Westernized cousins—again suggesting better education or healthier lifestyles. The US proponents for an "Obamacare"-style health service need to clearly weigh the cost implications, unless serious lifestyle changes occur (35).

What is worrying is that in the twenty-four–year duration of those WHO statistics, the Middle East has shown an increase from 6 million to 43 million diabetes sufferers. This period almost exactly equates with both the urbanization and expanding consumerism of those Middle Eastern nations. Westernization is bad for your health.

There are some things which cannot simply be controlled (or, at least, significantly diminished) by lifestyle. The incidence of waterborne diseases such as bilharzia in the tropics or Weil's disease in temperate zones provide such examples. The rising incidence (and cost) of dementia globally is yet to be realized, but could exceed that of diabetes health care! What needs to happen is both much stronger health education and the adoption of a religious vision which enables the quality of life, rather than longevity, to become the prevailing value in Westernized lifestyles.

Alternative currencies

To some degree, we are all naturally envious of those whose lives operate above subsistence level but within a "barter economy." US satellite TV channels, shown across the planet, are full of such examples, whether it is Alaskan homesteaders, Louisiana trappers, Scottish crofters, or Australian outbackers. In some senses, the Amish communities in America or so-called peasant farmers in southeast Asia operate barter economies on a regional scale; their sharing in communal barn-raisings or seed-sowing or harvesting demonstrate a voluntarism in sharing labor without reward.

One would labor and not ask for any reward, knowing that one day your neighbors would do the same on your project.

In some countries, cities and towns are allowed to create their own currencies; formally, these are known as local exchange trading systems. LETS operate alongside the countries' usual currency. As in the formal national currencies, a LETS is normally based on the most common paper unit, either US$ or UK£, which act as a promissory note.[10] I know of LETS in at least fourteen UK locations, where individuals can charge for their services in, e.g., "Stroud Pounds." In Bristol (England's sixth largest city), their LETS is so well established that both the mayor and the chief executive have chosen to be paid in "Bristol Pounds." LETS help develop a unity of common and local identity.

How we utilize housing creates another form of currency. Security in our home(land) or in our housing is a currency that we often ignore. How easily or well do we welcome friends, neighbors, and strangers for meals and as overnight guests?[11] We can use our homes as "beacons" of proto-community, which is a missionary action.[12] The needs of the poor and homeless are often threatened by insecurity and financial systems that favor the rich and/or landowning. How wrong is federal taxation that sides with the landlord or makes homeowning profitable via tax breaks?[13] In parts of the USA, Scandinavia, and Germany, long-term tenants are protected by statute or rent controls, providing family, community, and educational stability.

My understanding is that the jury is even further out on Bitcoin than it is on Adam Smith. Bitcoin is a digital currency, which can be transferred in "wallets" across the Internet without the intermediary of a bank or regulated financial institution.[14] Aaargh! Obviously, those who wish to transfer money without accountability, such as criminals or corrupt governments, favour Bitcoin because it keeps all such transactions below the radar. The fact that major US and UK banks are dedicating staff and resources to monitoring, if not servicing, Bitcoin tells how seriously its development is taken. But when another of the world's leading Bitcoin authorities refuses

---

10. Bang, *Ecovillages*, 211–16.

11. Pohl, *Making Room*.

12. Francis, *Hospitality and Community*.

13. Francis, ed., *Foxes Have Holes*, 114–16.

14. Popper, *Digital Gold*.

to invest more than US$500 in it,[15] it suggests there are major questions still to be asked and regulation needed if the "fast and furious" are not to profit from the poor. Bitcoin requires financial knowledge and good IT, further separating the haves from the have-nots, be it in education or technology, questioning whether this can be a "common good" longer-term development.

The global Internet and the exponential rise of personal technology (cell phones, etc.) are pulling the world into a new currency of information and/or communication. "Mobile phones and the Internet are ending the information famine of rural areas in Asia and Africa. Improved logistics now enable global industries to operate profitably in far-flung regions."[16] Knowledge is power—and those who have knowledge, however Machiavellian, and particularly knowledge denied to masses with search engines, have a currency to be feared. No wonder that, when such technology is used for nefarious and/or abusive purposes, it is known as the "dark net." It was a cause for personal rejoicing when former UK Chief Rabbi Jonathan Sacks was awarded the 2016 Templeton Prize (for religious advancement and corporate spiritual progress) for his advocacy of the Internet, in its creative possibility: "The power of the web to convey spirituality is something we are only just beginning to explore."[17] Such alternative currencies demonstrate the tension in technology that shows how it can be used for good or ill.

The worst form of alternative currency is the corporate barony (or "the suit," as one of my best friends terms it).

- Whether it is the unwitting collusion of companies that produce processed food and supermarket buyers to create the global horsemeat scandal of 2013 to profit at the expense of consumers . . .[18]

- Whether it is in VW-Audi's self-admitted but lengthy illegal deception of the global market, destroying its declared integrity and mechanical reliability . . .

- Whether it is in the UK Chancellor of the Exchequer (George Osborne)'s willingness to court multi-billion Chinese funding for

15. *Sunday Times,* August 8, 2015, *Money Section.*

16. Sachs, *End of Poverty,* 289.

17. Jonathan Sacks, quoted in *The Times* (UK) on March 5, 2016.

18. Francis, *What in God's Name?,* 10–14.

Britain's high-speed rail network in advance of its parliamentary agreement . . .

- Why is it when the US president and the Pope both call for international climate change measures to be implemented immediately, the world's media sneer with amusement and big business just carries on?

It is not a conspiracy theory to state that, in the world that we have inherited from the twentieth century, the transnational "moneymen" seek to rule for self-interest and profit without environmental conscience. They operate internationally without real accountability. These are people who seek to work under a mantle of respectability, political or commercial office by creating power blocs and trading treaties that exploit the world and its peoples—without real thought or any faithful vision for the next generation.

Power blocs and trading treaties

Any reader who was socially aware during 1962 of the Bay of Pigs crisis, as a focus of the Cold War between the USA and the Soviet bloc, will understand that international confederacies have to be monitored. Do the United States of Brazil question themselves in the same ways as the United States of America? Is it nations or transnational corporations that really benefit from the increasingly imposed TTIP regulations (29) upon northern hemisphere trade? How many of us really understand the global "reach" of corporations such as the USA's Cargill or Monsanto, India's TATA, South Korea's Hyundai, and Brazil's Petrobras or JBS? How does the world regulate such tentacular interests in favor of just distribution to all and reducing planetary costs?

What can begin life as a seeming philanthropically best-motivated gathering of nations may require increasing critique and formal review. A trivial example would be the alleged increasing corruption of FIFA, soccer's world governing body. A more serious example is the European Union. Prior to its 1992 Maastricht Treaty, it was predominantly a social union, fostering human rights and a European identity, nurturing tariff-free trading and creating healthy political dialogue. Since Maastricht, it has become increasingly federalized, with the advent of the euro as a (majority) common currency, increasing EU statutory veto over national legislative trajectories (including judicially), and creating greater freedom of citizen movement, all while increasing in size. There is an important Christian critique of the

EU to be developed as it appears to become yet another political power bloc shoving for position in the economic hierarchy of world nations.

My lifetime has witnessed both the demise of the USSR into separate republics and the Balkans crisis in the 1990s, when Western governments made ineffectual attempts peaceably to end the interreligious warfare that caused poverty and mass murder, having failed to learn the lessons of the Nigerian crisis and Asian wars of the 1960s. The USA must take responsibility in creating a global hierarchy of nations, which require twentieth-century economics to prevail. The now unattributable "Free trade, specialization and global integration means that nations are no longer free *not* to trade" statement increasingly appears within credible economic papers. History demonstrates that war becomes an almost inevitable consequence of protecting one's interests whether it already-accrued wealth or market interests.[19] "To avoid war, nations must both consume less and become more self-sufficient."[20] In other words, we must adopt such a simplicity of lifestyle that we gradually let go of global profit-driven interdependence.

But as the recent creation (by former President Obama and the Japanese prime minister) of the Trans-Pacific Partnership (TPP) reminds us, economic forces demanding such interdependence run counter to that simplicity of lifestyle. TPP involves twelve "Pacific Rim" nations, but not China, and encompasses 40 percent of the global economy. Such power blocs and trading treaties operate through self-interest and not the "reign of God."

Postcards from Taizé, Iona, and Compostela

I was in my teens when I first joined a group to travel to the ecumenical monastery at Taizé, in Burgundy, France. During the Second World War, its founding prior, Brother Roger, lived alone there, tending a vegetable garden and offering shelter to refugees. He escaped on foot during the night the Nazis arrived to arrest him. After the war, he was joined by other young men, both Protestant and Catholic, to form the ecumenical eponymous community, with its daily threefold times of corporate prayer, welcome to increasing numbers of pilgrims, and the publication of various brothers' writings and their modern-day multilingual chants.[21]

19. Kwarteng, *War and Gold*.
20. Daly, *Beyond Growth*, 157.
21. Gonzales-Balado, *Story of Taizé*.

Brother Roger, his spirituality, and his writings have been a profound influence upon my life. For several years, I used to take student groups annually to the huge tented summer gathering of young people. Together, we shared in the daily prayer, silence, study sessions, and socializing across many races and languages. The Taizé vision of a church and a world called to live as one was enriching and life-changing for everyone. Over the years, before Brother Roger's tragic 2005 murder (by a deranged woman) during worship, I was privileged to have three separate personal conversations with him—a great encouragement to understand ministry as an ecumenical catalyst. At Taizé, with its meals of Earth-friendly simplicity, mutual service, and learning, we knew the world "could be as one" if we learned to listen and live Jesus-style.[22]

Books from Taizé, whether Brother Roger's or others', and Taizé music are within arm's reach as I type. Two of his books traveled within my backpack as I went off to Iona for the first time, over forty years ago, on an ecumenical youth pilgrimage. There I found the roaring silence, vibrant songs and worship, mutual service, simple meals, and the same call to ecumenical resolve, as at Taizé. It has been Celtic, Anabaptist, and liberation theologies that have driven my theology but it has been their congregations' servant examples, as well as that of the Taizé and Iona Communities that have provided the beat of my ecumenical heart for shared spirituality and discipleship.

The contemporary Iona Community's founder George MacLeod once wrote:

> The cross must be raised again at the centre of the marketplace as well as on the steeple of the church. I am claiming that Jesus was not crucified in a cathedral between two candles, but on a cross between two thieves; on the town garbage heap, at a crossroads so cosmopolitan they had to write His title in Hebrew, Latin, and Greek. At the kind of place where cynics talk smut, and thieves curse, and soldiers gamble, because that is where He died and that is what He died about and that is where churchmen ought to be and what churchmen should be about.[23]

The failure of some of the UK's most well-known churches to cope with the camps of Occupy protesters outside their landmark buildings (such as St Paul's Cathedral, London) shows how far they are becoming removed from

22. Spink, *Universal Heart*.

23. MacLeod, *Only One Way Left*, 38.

identifiable servant communities. The response of churches in different US cities to the pamphleteering and other actions of the Occupy protestors says much about how those parts of the church see their role in society and their relationship to the state.

The church must recognize that it lives again at the margins of power and is a counterculture. The age of post-Christendom has dawned, more so in Europe than in the Americas. The church must learn how to be a vibrant servant community if it is to have any voice in the public square of contemporary debate.[24]

For some years, I lived in a French village next to one of the four starting points of *El Camino de Santiago*, running a small retreat house. Often, we played initial host for those gathering themselves for the long walk ahead to Compostela in Spain. I easily recall several conversations with such pilgrims, both Christian and not, about how this was going to be a "walk of reflection" to wrestle with life's big questions. In my occasional accompanying hikes in both France and Spain, conversation on the road recognized how much local congregations would have to change to emulate the hospitality and servant heart of the hosts of our overnight *pensiones*.

Wrestling with God's intentions

As this book is published, I am gathering and reediting my notes for another book about how Christians individually and the servant communities (of which they must become part) are "wrestling towards a blessing."[25] Whether it is in the limping away of Jacob from Jabbok (Gen 32:22ff) or Mary's "ponderings" (Luke 1:38; 2:51; John 19:25ff) or ours today, we are called to wrestle with God's intention in order to receive blessing.

In the Hebrew people, God chose a nation that struggled with its destiny and was often oppressed. In Jesus, God spoke to the world through its marginalized edges, which included speaking like a Galilean. Perhaps God does mean faith to be a counterculture, prophetically questioning mainstream self-interests and living as servant communities. "The prophetic consciousness of Moses, the Hebrew prophets, and Jesus dares to imagine another way to live and structure society."[26]

24. Williams, *Faith in the Public Square*.
25. Francis, *Wrestling towards a Blessing* (forthcoming).
26. Friesen, *Artists, Citizens, Philosophers*, 205.

In John 17, the writer records Jesus as wrestling in prayer. Part of his intercession with his heavenly parent is in seeking ways in which his life and impending death may draw his disciples, as representatives of all God's people, together to live and act as one. If this was God's intention in those moments of his incarnation and ultimate revelation, why should we reject that "to be as one" intention now?

This poses huge challenges to humankind as this chapter has begun to outline. God does not want and we cannot afford a world in which the rich take "the lion's share" of Earth's resources, including food, and also demand ever-increasing health care provision while allowing the corporate barony of the transnationals to rule our lives at the expense of both the majority and the poor. That is not "at one."

We have to learn how we bring the complementary challenges of economy, ecology, and ecumeny together "as one." We need to be living and sharing within the prophetic vanguard of a community that believes in that "at one" theology. While the postcards and the signposts to others may be important encouragement, it is only when our own spirituality and discipleship incorporate (some would say "incarnate") such "at one-ness" that the world might believe.

9 Spirituality and Discipleship

Jesus-shaped spirituality and discipleship are at the heart of vibrant Christian faith—both at an individual level and as a community of believers. Jesus said: "Blessed are the pure in heart, for they shall see God" (Matt 5:8). "To cultivate that purity of heart is the work of the inner life that, alone, can hold our lives in right relationship. It is why humankind cannot live by bread alone."[1] Jesus did not talk of fundamentalism or extremism or advocate violence but encouraged everyone towards the radical egalitarianism of the "reign of God."[2]

I have had a rich life traveling among radical Christians. As a blessed teenager, I lived in one of Birmingham's international Selly Oak Colleges, daily worshiping, eating, and living among others from around the world. Later, I sat at Amish tables and outside the home of a Greek Orthodox shepherd for meals, only eating what they had grown, reared, or baked. I have worked with North American Mennonites, creating vegetable gardens, teaching groups, and developing study materials. I have been invited to teach in ecumenical student chaplaincies, Quaker retreat houses, at Greenbelt[3] as well as other festivals, and at Iona Abbey. I have led groups to Israel's Tantur Ecumenical Centre, annually leading a student pilgrimage to Taizé's summer camp in France, and I have taken groups to a Franciscan *pensione* close to Vatican City and the Waldensian study center high

---

1. McIntosh, *Rekindling Community*, 54.

2. Francis, *Shalom*, 27–28.

3. Like the similar annual festivals of Solas in Scotland and the Wild Goose Festival in the USA.

up in the Italian mountains, as well as having walked with fellow pilgrims along parts of *El Camino de Santiago* in Spain. Every encounter was unique and encouraging—their Christian spirituality was enriching their daily discipleship, as we all shared in others' hospitality, learning, prayer, and conversation together.

My partner, Janice, and I love returning to the Scottish island of Iona, where in AD 597 the Irish monk Columba arrived to continue planting Christianity across Scotland. The modern-day Iona Community runs a residential, short-burst teaching program there. Their commitment to the "reign of God," "Earth-friendly" living, justice, and peace, as well as Celtic spirituality, provides rich inspiration for everyday discipleship.[4] "The issue . . . is not whether Celtic spirituality ever existed but the fact that a living spirituality connecting soil, soul and society manifestly can and does exist."[5] We carry that life within us back into our city home and neighborhood.

Celtic, Amish, Quaker, Mennonite, Orthodox, Taizé, or Franciscan are simply different expressions of vibrant Christian faith, which each find spirituality and discipleship as the two facets of the soul's journey like a spinning coin through life. What binds these different expressions together is their integrity in bringing economy, ecology, and community (ecumeny) together in their respective vibrancy. What we do today and how we live now is determined by our vision of God's world, whatever tomorrow or next year may bring.

Blade Runner vs. *Star Trek*

I remember vividly the minicab driving across the causeway through the Balinese mangrove swamp to our hotel. We passed palm-thatched huts, lit by kerosene lamps, but the main light came from giant TV screens showing *Star Trek*. Gene Roddenberry's über-American vision of future peace-desiring, galactic missions were global in their repeated TV showings and spin-off films.

As seminarians, we rather abandoned *Star Trek* in favor of Ridley Scott's 1982 dystopian film, *Blade Runner*. Set in Los Angeles in 2019, technology had created androids or replicant humans, for work in the space colonies. Those replicants were hunted down by the blade runner. It was a

---

4. Shanks, *IONA*.

5. McIntosh, *Soil and Soul*, 18.

far more frightening future scenario than ever *Star Trek* posited. I will not spoil your enjoyment by telling you more of *Blade Runner*'s plot.

Time waits for no one . . .

Blade Runner was based upon Philip K. Dick's 1968 novel *Do Androids Dream of Electric Sheep?*, throwing his narrative over fifty years or two generations into the future—to 2018. As this book is published (2017), we live in a world of robots, genomics, bionic limbs, androids, and amazing surgery. Because of removed heavy cataracts, I now read this text through artificial eye-lens implants. But we are far more than a year or so away from replicants that are indistinguishable from humans and the political nightmares of maverick "blade runners" in Los Angeles.

However we now live in a world of such fast technological change and developments in artificial intelligence that humankind will struggle to keep up.[6] We only need to realize the struggles of indigenous peoples across the world in their encounters with Christianized Westerners—as "we" challenged them and their centuries-old lifestyles to adapt to us, our economic ways, and technological advances in decades rather than generations—to realize this. That pace of change has accelerated over the recent centuries.

In 1717, it was easy for Westerners to predict that their world in 1750 would not be that dramatically different. In 1817, steam locomotion and mechanization was in its infancy. Who could have predicted that, by 1850, the European Industrial Revolution would have so exponentially grown that steam trains were being considered to open up frontiers in America, Asia, and the Russias? In 1917—the year of the Russian Revolution—who could have predicted the growth of either the Communist system or the USA's capitalist economic dominance by 1950, and how that would create such enmities? Now in 2017 . . . who can predict the world of 2050, given that so much of humankind's present indecision, rather than its invention, may threaten or even cause human (and other) life to cease on planet Earth?

Living prophetically

As Christians, we have to understand that we cannot predict the future but we can live prophetically now, taking account of the best scientific

6. Harari, *Homo Sapiens.*

know-how, economic practices, and "Earth-friendly" lifestyles to enable the planet and all its/God's people to share more equally in its future.

Biblical prophecy is not "telling the future" like some mystic charlatan in a fairground or roadside booth. Biblical prophecy is reminding people that unless we live as God intends, both we as individuals, and communities or nations, will separate ourselves from the divine purpose. That is what the message of Micah, Amos, Isaiah, Malachi, and all the other biblical prophets is about. Follow the manufacturer's instructions—if you want the best use of what is provided. In biblical language, follow the Creator's intentions, as supremely revealed in Jesus, if you want to live fully and fairly within God's *oikos*.

Living prophetically is a matter of spirituality and discipleship. It is not about extremism or right-wing theology—but it is radical and Jesus-shaped. Economically, it will mean living with less expectation of future (or even any) growth and much less possession or (mis)usage of things and resources. Ecologically, it will mean living an Earth-friendly lifestyle, reducing our consumption, cooperatively sharing as much as possible, and treading "lightly upon the planet." Ecumenically, there is an even bigger challenge as we learn to act as a global community, respecting each other's differences and divergences while creating a new nonthreatening interdependence. If you are uncertain, ask yourself whether Isaiah 11:6 is a metaphor or a prophetic promise.

Contemplation in a world of action

For many years, I was joyfully encouraged by the many writings of Thomas Merton, a Trappist monk who became a global spiritual teacher, partly because of his deep respect for other faiths' insights, particularly Buddhists. Like them, Merton believed that the integration of spirituality, nonviolent action, economic simplicity, and Earth-friendly lifestyle were at the heart of discipleship. Often a Merton book was on my bedside table; a particular favorite was his *Contemplation in a World of Action*, which complemented my Christian activism.

I was equally challenged by the similar integrity of values within the life and theology of the German academic and activist, Dorothee Soelle.[7] She challenged everyone's personal Christian vision and reflection away from Westernized individualism towards servant discipleship,

7. Francis, *Dorothee Soelle.*

which cohered within a community of praxis; that is, action and reflection (contemplation).

What I learned from these practical theologians and the radical Christian communities mentioned at the start of this chapter is that true spirituality and discipleship are indivisible. The way we live now and the nature of our economic priorities, ecological simplicity, relationships with others, and the integrity of all these together within our Christian faith speaks to those who live around (and with) us. But to live like this demands a contentment or inner peace, which can stem only from a quiet (rather than a restless) heart. Contemplatives have something to learn from activists just as activists must learn from contemplatives.

Prayer and meditation

Ruether's *Integrating Ecofeminism, Globalisation and World Religions* shows how the world is on a disintegrative path economically, ecologically, and sociologically. Ruether's thesis is that the prayer, spirituality, and lifestyle of religious followers (disciples, in Christian terms) are creating the inner resources as necessary exemplars to take others around them on an alternative course towards a creative coherence.

For many world religions, such inner resources are centered within regular or daily prayer and meditation. To focus upon that which is holy, that is of the divine, enables one to become more integrated in both the divine intention and that *oikos* that is of God. The Hindu's Bhagavid Gita teaches: "Though a man be soiled with the sins of a lifetime, let him but love me, rightly resolved in utter devotion; I see no sinner, that man is holy."[8] Is this not akin to redemption through grace?

Personally, I find more affinity with many Sikhs and Hindus, with their more flexible ethical code interpretations, than with the more extreme or violent followers of Abrahamic faiths. But what does Jesus invite his disciples to be? Space precludes full discussion here of the human demands of the Beatitudes or his teaching in the enveloping Sermon on the Mount (Matt 5–7), such as "Blessed are the pure in heart, for they shall see God" (Matt 5:8). The Bhagavid Gita's "By lust, by avarice, by anger is the atman

---

8. There are several authentic translations of the Bhagavid Gita, from the Sanskrit, but they "arrive" without chapter-and-verse referencing; this quote is from the section about mysticism.

hidden"[9] could almost be a comment upon that Beatitude; our earthly vices separate us from God's intention. The Jewish zealot or Islamist militant, who perceive violence against the innocent as rewarded in "heaven," are further away from my (and many others') understanding of the divine intention.

Christian humility and meditation of our own traditions' Scripture requires a discipline of prayer. Just as I would not be without our discipleship group's fortnightly meal, I would not be without the silent contemplation and compline[10] of my weekly meditation group. Nurturing the right attitude of heart towards God, the creation, and our fellow human beings is common to all faith communities. For us all, that is gradually accomplished by frequent prayer and meditation.

Paradise lost? Paradise gained . . .

I recall the palpable shock among the young people gathered at a church conference when my cohost (now a pastor in Australia) and I answered a teenager's questions in complementary ways. We were asked, "What happens if there is nothing more when we die and won't you feel cheated?" No. My colleague and I both affirmed, and agreed, that even if there was no "afterlife" *per se*, we still would have wanted to be Christians (followers of Jesus) in this earthly life, because of the spirituality and discipleship we had enjoyed, the communities of faith we had been enriched by, and the vision for everyday living which that faith provided.

For the Victorian preacher and even unthinking contemporary evangelicals, the ability to dangle listening sinners over the fiery pit of hell helped drive up their conversion rates. Conversion to what? Increased fear of an unmerciful God? I struggle to reconcile the idea of the One-ness of a Triune God with the thought of Jesus giving an unequivocal welcome, and his Father in heaven being about to condemn those who fall short of the Spirit's leading. The sandwich view of the universe with its hell below and heaven above should have disappeared from both faithful and logical thinking with Galileo's and Newton's help and discoveries. However, I can see how the jihadist can be encouraged unto death by the concept of "paradise" where ultimate pleasures are promised. Ideas of heaven and hell

9. The *atman* is the eternal soul of the individual self; it is this which makes each human being unique in the sight of God.

10. A formal pattern of corporate late-evening or night prayer.

are part of both Christianity and Islam—but in different ways and with very different descriptions.

Throughout my life, I have been greatly helped by the developing Hebrew, or Jewish, view of the "afterlife." Clearly the Hebrew testament refers to a "netherworld"—"If I make my bed in *Sheol,* Thou art there" (Ps 139:8). It is important to note that *Sheol* is not a place of divine punishment but a place of divine presence, where there is no separation from God. Over the centuries, rabbis have acknowledged *Sheol* as a way of comforting the bereaved but focused their teaching upon living within God's intention in this earthly life.

For some, who wanted evil people to be punished, the Hebrew concept of a "burning hell" arrived. This was called *Gehinnon* or *Gehenna,* which was the name of the putrid rubbish tip with its spontaneous fires, just south of the Jerusalem from Jesus' earthly days. But good Jewish theology taught that no one consigned to *Gehenna* would remain there for more than a year, thus making "hell" in Jewish thinking a temporary concept. This is far removed from the later corrupted Christian and Islamic thinking of "eternal separation from God" or the everlasting fires of damnation. The Jewish *Gehenna* is also far removed from the lives of those peoples in the developing world who live their lives on toxic and putrid rubbish tips, scavenging and recycling for their *whole* lifetime, and not just a year of such "hell."

For those latter folk, I would want (if not need) a spirituality and discipleship in my life and those of other Westernized believers that provides me with a vision of a God-intended world, in which no one must live by such scavenging. Why? Because God's vision is one in which we all share all that is provided and no one expects the rest to live on our scraps, waste, and refuse. Having read the biblical creation narratives, the Hebrew prophets and the Gospels, as well as Milton and Dante, I see that both "hell" and eternal separation from God's intention is a matter of our human choices—for us personally as well as others in this world. The African child who dies of starvation does so because of western insularity and greed—and this is not God's intention, as "we" create that hell for them.

Within Islam, the concept of paradise is the promised final dwelling place for the faithful. The Qu'ran recognizes the hell of that starving African child too, calling Muslims to make this earthly world a foretaste of the paradise to come. It is exciting to understand that faithful, orthodox Islam both honors creation and its long-term well-being, meaning that their understanding of "paradise" as an idyllic garden of delights is predicated upon it being even better than the best of earthly creation.

Eco-Muslims recognize that the Qu'ran deplores the potential of the future hole in the ozone layer: "And we made the sky a protected ceiling [or 'canopy'], but they, from its signs are turning away" (Q. 21:32). Right from the outset of Muslim thought, there is respect for the creation of Allah/God: ". . . and do not commit abuse on the earth, spreading corruption" (Q. 2:60). English does not serve the Arabic "corruption" well, as the Arabic meaning includes not only bad economic practices or inadequate community but also creating homelessness and damaging the earth's goodness/integrity. Thoughtful Islam has a great understanding for both "treading lightly upon the Earth" and creating an economy that sustains the world and its peoples with justice. "The Qu'ran teaches that the act of destroying or spreading ruin on this earth is one of the gravest sins possible—*fasad fi al-ard*, which means to corrupt the Earth by destroying the beauty of creation, is considered an ultimate act of blasphemy against God" (Q. 2:190 and elsewhere).[11] Spirituality and justice intertwine within orthodox Islam, too.

Within the Abrahamic faiths, one's personal understanding of "paradise" (or its alternative) is determined by visionary spirituality and earthly discipleship, which, in their turn, determine the kind of servant communities of faith that we belong to.

Servant communities

My *kibbutz* experiences have been few and short-term, but there was always a clear sense of communal servanthood among the adult members, whether we were working a vegetable garden or on a building project. I have been a guest, led or spent retreats in Benedictine, Carmelite, Franciscan, and Ignatian houses—all part of historic Western monasticism—where the discipline of the resident community was clearly a call to servanthood, not just to us as guests but to each other as Christian sisters and brothers.

One of my great joys is staying with the modern-day Iona Community, on the sacred Scottish island. Whether as a guest or a visiting enabler/teacher, I rejoice that we share many domestic chores each day alongside our prayer, pilgrimage, and learning. There is something life-enhancing about chopping the morning's vegetables for later meals, cleaning the

11. Abou El Fadl, *Great Theft*, 130.

bathrooms, or washing-up after communal bedtime drinks, in that shared servanthood.

The Archbishop of Canterbury, Justin Welby, at his "enthronement" (can we change this idea, please?) declared that his two main priorities for the worldwide Anglican Community would be prayer and restoring spirituality to the heart of discipleship. Acting prophetically, he set up the Community of St Anselm,[12] in which sixteen young (predominantly professional) people would make a ten-month commitment to live together in London's Lambeth Palace. While pursuing their daily professions, they would also share in daily prayer, communal meals, and periods of study, and spend one third of their "free" time serving in various Christian charities, including homeless shelters and refugee centers. They will be joined in this year-long profession by a further twenty similar young people who will be nonresidential. The aim is to provide each year's community with the spirituality and discipleship to have the tools to encourage, influence, and change the lives of others in the future. Their future servanthood *should* be generous, Jesus-shaped, and of help to those around them (and with whom they work) to question the way the world works—and doesn't—for the common good.

One of the few facts commonly known about the Amish, other than horse-drawn buggies and their seeming rejection of technological advance, is that they share in "barn raisings" communally. Through such shared commitments and desire for traditional forms of peaceable community, "the moral order of Amish culture also places many restraints on economic life."[13] This means that in the Amish community's adaptation to twenty-first–century life, land pressures, and its rising costs, they are developing small-scale, often agrarian- or craft-oriented family-run businesses.[14] This is driven by Amish thrift, Christian stewardship, and a desire to serve the needs of their neighbors, while witnessing to innate discipleship and spirituality. "The Amish remind us that, in the final analysis, technology and economic practice ought to be designed and deployed to serve the long-term interests of the common good of human communities."[15]

During theologian Dorothee Soelle's South American travels, she noted the marked contrast between the natural cooperation within Latin

12. www.stanselm.org.uk.

13. Kraybill, "Amish Economics," 84.

14. Kraybill and Nolt, *Amish Enterprise.*

15. Kraybill, "Amish Economics," 88.

American settlements and the Western consumerism of her academic tenured locations: "All participate in the communal work . . . the reputation of persons in these settlements is not determined by their attitude towards money but by their sense of responsibility to the whole."[16] A similar vision was held by the Simple Way community, who set themselves up in a Kensington district rowhouse in Philadelphia (where else?), where they fed the hungry, ran a thrift store, and planted vegetable gardens.[17] In 2009, Berea Mennonite Church (near Atlanta, Georgia) created Oakleaf Mennonite Farm on its own nine-acre lot, to provide locally grown food to their immediate community, who had no neighborhood food stores. "Berea hopes to be a model of an alternative society that is built upon fresh fair food that nourishes the bodies and the spirits of those gathered. This is a witness to those outside the church."[18]

In the UK, the Sheffield Inner City Ecumenical Mission similarly set up community houses, a credit union, a food cooperative, and the Urban Theology Unit.[19] While serving as executive vice-chair of the UK's Mennonite Trust, I rejoiced that in our then north London center and later in a temporary Birmingham staff house, we had vegetable gardens; our "green thumbs," the produce, and the home-cooked meals shared with guests told of our life together as a serving community. In Oxford, the tiny Littlemore Baptist Church sacrificed its own large chapel to enable the building of apartments for those newly emerging from long-term social care—thanks to a prayerful, visionary leadership.[20] In the large town where I live, an ecumenical parish uses its buildings to host a community-run café, a food bank warehouse (distributing commodities to destitute families), a furniture restoration business charity staffed by unemployed folks, recovering alcoholics, and others with mental health issues, as well as hosting three different worshiping congregations. Spirituality and discipleship grow together.

As Satish Kumar, the Jain peace and environmental activist, often teaches: "Right thinking is to think well of others and put the well-being of others, before your own."[21] Was it not Jesus who took up the towel and wa-

16. Soelle, *Celebrating Resistance*, 37–38.

17. Claiborne, *Irresistible Revolution*.

18. Werner, "Peace and Agriculture," 78.

19. Vincent, *Into the City*.

20. Francis, ed., *Foxes Have Holes*, 28.

21. Kumar, *Soil, Soul, Society*, 51.

ter to wash his own disciples' feet? On both sides of the Atlantic, I have sung Richard Gillard's excellent hymn, "Brother, Sister, Let Me Serve You . . ." and wondered whether everyone in those congregations really understand the implications of what they were singing. "Christian spirituality proposes an alternative understanding of the quality of life, and encourages a prophetic and contemplative lifestyle, one capable of deep enjoyment, free of the obsession with consumption . . . Christian spirituality proposes a growth marked by moderation and the capacity to be happy with little. It is a return to that simplicity . . . ."[22]

Chlopski filosof

From my twenties, in each decade of my adult life, I have tried to learn something of another language and its native culture. During my fifties, I have wrestled somewhat abortively with Polish and Russian: recurring bouts of hospitalization prevented travel and denied attendance at language classes. But I have learned enough from conversation in my local *Polski sklep* (grocery store) to know of the role and wisdom of the *chlopski filosof* within Polish village communities.

Literally, *chlopski filosof* translates as a "peasant-philosopher." Often these are devout, well-read, and prayerful Roman Catholics who earn their living locally, either on the land or in artistic roles, such as musicians, icon painters, or instrument makers. But their greater significance is in their role and authority as wise interpreters of religious truths, who often act as mentors for the young or talented and as mediators between neighbors in dispute with each other. It is a grassroots movement with neither hierarchy nor organization. Lots of societies, which western sophistication or academic snobbery call primitive, have such wise men (or women) in their midst.

Every society needs a *chlopski filosof* who can act as a wise counterpoint to both religious and political establishments. They become oral purveyors of the "currency of ideas," so necessary in this age of disposable e-books, growing political expediencies, economic instabilities, eco-crises, and religious extremisms. When that peasant philosophy is embodied in the integrity of the prayer and spirituality of someone local, whose wisdom and integrity is respected by those in the surrounding community,

22. Francis, *Laudato Si'*, para. 222, 105.

the world can risk the life-giving decentralization that the world crises are pushing us towards.

Keith Hebdon, who is director of the Urban Theology Unit, has a ministry of facilitating urban communities, which has led him to observe that such "Community leaders are rarely politically ambitious because their ambition is for their community. Identifying grassroots leadership is a tricky task . . . especially for those of us with a middle class model of leadership . . . . [Such] local leaders are the seeds of change, scattered broadly among the community . . . they then begin to draw others into the urge to transform unjust structures."[23] This is also the way of the *chlopski filosov* . . . just as it is the way of Jesus.

Unfortunately, just as the British used to make jokes about the Irish, so Statesiders are going to have to abandon making jokes about Poles or their supposed stupidity, if we are to learn from their gifts, such as *chlopski filosof*. But vitally, this is also about the gospel where it is in the seeming weakness of the incarnation that we discover the wisdom and strength of the eternal God.

23. Hebden, *Seeking Justice*, 96.

AND SO . . .

10 "Towards a New Vision for All God's People . . ."

One of the almost forgotten pop artists was DianeL, but, once seen, her work "Common Skin" could never be forgotten. She had fashioned a huge amoeba-like coat from a shiny, red plasticized material, with full body and head-hooding for eleven people. Wherever her art was shown around the world, she carried "Common Skin" with her in a suitcase, then persuaded passers-by to put it on while others gave out leaflets for her show. At first each group of eleven flailed around wildly but slowly they gained a composure, a common identity and then direction as they walked together, like a creature from some post-apocalyptic dream. This artwork increasingly gained meaning as more watchers began to move on from its initial antisexist protest towards the fact that we all share a common skin, whatever our race and gender, and it is only by moving in a commonly shared direction that humankind can have forward movement—and therefore a future.

Artists, citizens, philosophers

Unless we make deliberate choices to live in hermitical solitude or in isolated family groups (often on rural livestock stations), most folks congregate together, for example, whether as Nenet herders, Alaskan homesteaders, or Indonesian villagers, or in varying sized settlements, up to vast conurbations. From the 2000s, more than 50 percent of people live in large cities rather than in smaller towns or rural areas—for the first time in global history. Any reputable search engine can produce a reliable list of global cities by population size. The overwhelming majority of those with over ten million inhabitants are part of the BRIC and MINT nations (23); regrettably, urbanization, overpopulation, and economic growth frequently codevelop. The prophetic (and I would affirm Christian) voice must ask two questions:

1. Can ongoing economic growth even be desirable in the face of growing environmental concerns?

2. How can we ensure a good quality of life for *every* resident of such large, growing cities and for those of *all* races *and* species who live within their hinterland?

The concept of the city is essential to the biblical trajectory. In the Mosaic code, six cities were designated as "cities of refuge," where peaceable relations and true justice must prevail (Josh 20). Of all the prophets, Jeremiah is most explicit that the faithful believer must "seek the welfare of the city" (Jer 29:7). Jesus wept over the city of Jerusalem, because of its inhabitants' unfaithfulness to God's reign and intention for human living. The first Christian mission spread out from major urban centers, along trading routes (Acts). The book of Revelation tells of a "a new heaven and a new earth" exemplified by a renewed city, with the river of life flowing through it, where the trees of plenty shed the leaves of peace (Rev 22).[1] Early in my ministry, I was greatly helped by reading the work of and also attending a residential seminar addressed by Ray Bakke,[2] a renowned city missiologist. Subsequent courses at Sheffield's Urban Theology Unit,[3] as well as my friendship with and the writings of Stuart Murray,[4] affirmed my consequent calling to city-styled ministries.

I love cities. To enjoy time, friends, and conversation among the galleries, "street theater," coffee- and book-shops of Christiania in Copenhagen, Leith in Edinburgh, Moseley in Birmingham (UK), Paris's Left Bank, central Amsterdam, and Balboa Park, San Diego, are memories to relive if not repeat. Yet urban pollution and traffic emissions mean that because of a chronic heart condition, I am now having to move away from cities and visit them for short periods only. I am extremely aware that the ways

1. Interestingly, the Iroquois, Oneida, and other native American peoples have legendary stories from their beginnings about the "tree of peace" being necessary for the gathering of their peoples, too.

2. Bakke, *Urban Christian.*

3. Vincent, *Into the City.*

4. Murray, *Challenge of the City.*

in which humankind lives and gathers together are threatening our very breathing. We live as captives in the gardens of our own making. To walk the waterfront boulevards of Vientiane or Saigon, Bordeaux, Sydney, and Chicago and know both shade and sun on your face makes it good to be alive. This is about the quality of life for us all. One of my favorite books is *Artists, Citizens, Philosophers*, by Duane Friesen, a Mennonite theologian who picks up on the fact that all human settlements of any size must have artists, citizens, and philosophers for the common good of all those who share in that community's life.

Perhaps a little more biographical information will help illustrate this. Part of being a responsible citizen (for me) is being involved in various pieces of voluntary work and community action, as well as being an active advocate of and worker at my own rented community garden. I also served on our local high school board, where our main thoroughfare has four significant pieces of sculpture, each ten feet (three meters) tall, leading to four color-coded classroom wings, each with their own gallery/display space and "cloth banners." I have several friends who work as artists, writers, potters, and musicians, living on the edge of cities, painting, producing, or performing, while teaching or enabling others with similar artistic gifts. "The arts help us overcome the numbing effect of a culture where the preciousness of life is taken for granted as we preserve 'our way of life' at the expense of others."[5] Art and culture help to enrich humanity, and Christian communities need to encourage such work.

How we interrelate as citizens and faith communities is vital to the holism of the town or city where we live. Faith communities have huge responsibility in both encouraging and enabling their neighborhood's residents to serve as responsible citizens to each other and to celebrate the nature of our common life. "Christians will participate in the building of a 'global civic culture.' They will seek to build a worldwide citizens' movement of peacemakers and peace-making groups . . . . The first step the church must take is to repent and be what we are called to be. Then we might be able to contribute as citizens to the peace of the city."[6] Helping ourselves, then our neighbors to understand the city, or whatever size neighborhood as one *oikos*, one household, which needs to live and work together for the common good, is a creative part of the biblical vision.

5. Friesen, *Artists, Citizens, Philosophers*, 205.
6. Ibid., 248–51.

Alongside others, I have lobbied successfully for the provision of children's playgrounds, for urban parks to be retained (rather than sold for development), for cycle paths, and for the expansion of community garden (allotment) schemes; all these are vital to our shared human well-being in urban settings.[7] In different locations as a pastor, I have co-organized the funding of new cooperative home-based businesses. "The Christian life must be expressed in the symbols, stories, myths, rituals and aesthetic forms and types of social organisation where the Church dwells."[8] Incarnational theology and *oikos* are closely interrelated—both cohere around the concept of "indwelling." The church is called to vocalize in corporate worship, activist discipleship, contemplative prayer, and humble-yet-demonstrable commitments to that "indwelling" which is of the *oikos* of God.

Over the years, I have met several urban-based Muslim scholars and moderate imams who obviously respect Jeremiah's "seek the welfare of the city" theology, as practically and liturgically expressed by Jewish and Christian faith communities. But both these latter must "go the extra mile" and actively encourage their public theologians, bishops, and senior rabbis first to become conversant in Arabic, then second (not secondarily) to engage Islamic scholars, mullahs, and imams in a new nonviolent and nonextremist reading of the Qu'ran. It is only when the vast majority of Muslims stop supporting Islamist extremism, whether by apathy, acceptance, education, or finance, that the barbaric violence of those jihadis will be starved out of existence by lack of wider support, as well as condemnation at international level. For the *oikos* of God to become a true reality, all Abrahamic faith communities will need to lobby governments, across the world, to stop that work of violence, resist harboring offenders and become the peacemakers that Jesus and Muhammad call the faithful believer to be.

"By the rivers of Babylon . . ."

We must learn from the accepted theological wisdom of Stanley Hauerwas and William Willimon to live as "resident aliens,"[9] living lightly and reactively to the idolatrous calls for nationalist or even "city-ist" identities. We must "seek the welfare of the city" for "at the centre of the Christian life

7. Woolley, *Urban Open Spaces.*

8. Friesen, *Artists, Citizens, Philosophers,* 277.

9. Hauerwas and Willimon, *Resident Aliens.*

is the call to discipleship, the call to follow the way of Jesus Christ and to embody that way of life in an alternative community: the Church."[10]

For the New Testament writers, "Babylon" was loose code for Rome (Rev 17–18)—the symbol of mainstream culture, violence, oppression, and the politico-economic system. The church was genuinely countercultural and nonviolent, therefore an "alternative community." To messianic Jews (those who had become Christians), the psalmist's lament had come true for it was by their *own* "rivers of Babylon" that they were indeed sitting down and weeping as they recalled the vision of Zion. That holy city of Revelation stood out as the alternative community for all against the worldly power and influence of Rome/"Babylon."

Sachs, the economist, wrote: "Our generation's greatest challenges—in environment, demography, poverty and global politics—are also our most exciting opportunities . . . . Ours is the generation that can harness science and a new ethic of global co-operation to bequeath a healthy planet to future generations . . . . Sustainable development will be achieved through global co-operation across nations, institutions and intellectual disciplines."[11] That is why this book makes a plea to integrate economic, ecological, and ecumenical thinking. It does so from radical Christian faith perspectives, rooting its challenge in the reforging of theology (or God-talk), to provide a coherent Jesus-shaped voice in the debate of the public square.

This becomes vital as we consider the increasing interdependence of nations. In the mid-2010s, China flooded the world with cheap steel—sold at far lower prices than any western company could produce it. This caused the Indian-based Tata conglomerate to close all its UK steel plants, devastating several towns' economies and most of their residents' livelihoods. Pittsburgh—all over again. Meanwhile China was investing financially all over Europe, predominantly in agriculture and infrastructure projects. In 2014, China invested US$5.1bn in the UK, US$3.5bn in Italy, US$2.3bn in the Netherlands, US$2bn in Portugal, and approximately US$1bn in several other European countries, as well as more in African, Australasian, and Latin American regions.[12] In 2015, figures rose to US$7.7bn for the UK and (at publication) are not yet verifiable for these other named areas, with an expected US$10bn-plus in the UK for 2016. Christians need to have done their homework before naming names.

10. Friesen, *Artists, Citizens, Philosophers*, 64.

11. Sachs, *Commonwealth*, 339–41.

12. Figures supplied by Baker and Mackenzie, profusion financial analysts, 2016.

As of 2016, an increasing public debate was beginning in the UK, augmented by voices from Europe. Senior politicians, eco-lobbying groups, energy companies, and security experts were questioning the wisdom to allow a new economic superpower to have so much influence, and even control, of vital industries and resources. Whether this was basic xenophobia or a sensible policy review is too early to judge; the detailed answers and broader judgement will not be known until years ahead. But it is a matter of discipleship to ask who is *now* the "whore of Babylon" (Rev 17:3), selling her wares of entrapment to gain long-term influence.

Perpetual growth cannot form part of any wise and appropriate agenda on a finite planet. Yet twentieth-century economics assume that ongoing growth is normative. "Green economics is all about sustainability and social justice: funding and sustaining such means of creating wealth will allow us to meet the genuine needs of all people without damaging our fragile biosphere."[13] From his UK perspective, economics professor Tim Jackson's 2011 compellingly argued book, *Prosperity without Growth: Economics for a Finite Planet* reveals its thesis in its title. Less accessible, but globally more influential, Christian Felber's 2015 *Change Everything: Economics for the Good*[14] eponymously shares its thesis. When renowned economists, such as Sachs, Daly, and Jackson, and the dominant voices of faith communities start to speak coherently and counterculturally against the vested interests of industrialists and corporate multinationals, it is time to check the counterculture—again. I believe that hindsight will teach us that the beginning of this third millennium saw the flowering of a "new" green economics school of thought. The names of Piketty, Schumacher, Scott Cato,[15] and Stiglitz[16] should be added to those already named in this is paragraph as the nine-strong vanguard of such thinkers.

Creating a community of visionary *oikos* thinking

Before the Second World War, a group of disparate academics and friends in Oxford, England, used to meet weekly together. They included *The Lord of the Rings* writer J. R. R. Tolkien, the populist theologian C. S. Lewis, and the poet-philosopher Owen Barfield. They became known as the "Inklings,"

13. Porritt, *Seeing Green*, 126.
14. Felber, *Change Everything*.
15. Scott Cato, *Environment and Economy*.
16. Stiglitz, *Stiglitz Report*.

weekly reading their academic papers and prospective writings and debating how their vision of the world fitted together. Another member was Charles Williams, a writer, poet, and lay theologian who developed the understanding of co-inherence.[17] This theory developed the interdependence of economy, ecology, and community (ecumeny) within the boundaries of what Earth could sustain. How often in all the Inklings' disparate writing and poetry do we see that ideal being proclaimed? Think of Tolkien's Middle Earth reflections or Lewis's Narnia and *Silent Planet* musings. But what is also key is that the Inklings mediated and cross-fertilized each other's writings via their weekly meetings. Sharing in a currency of ideas is vital.

> But it is a matter of hard fact, and not fiction, that the world can be envisioned differently. The rich world today is so vastly rich. An effort to end extreme poverty that would have seemed out of reach even a generation or two ago is now well within reach because the costs are now such a small fraction of the vastly expanded income of the rich world. Especially for the United States . . . the rich can manage to pay for a significant proportion of what needs to be done, either through a modest increase in taxation or a burst of large-scale philanthropy, commensurate with their vast wealth.[18]

World-respected economists like Sachs, Daly, Jackson, and Piketty can cogently, academically, and coherently argue for zero economic growth, as well as the ending of poverty and living sustainably within Earth's resources. It should not surprise us that Sachs and Daly (with theologian John Cobb) have published works with titles like *Commonwealth: Economics for a Crowded Planet* or *For the Common Good*, respectively.

The work of faith communities

Orthodox Islam indicts its believers to care for those who cannot care for themselves; "but you do not honour the orphan" (Q. 89:17). Remember that almsgiving (Arabic: *zakat*) is not just a demand but one of the five pillars of Islam. This echoes mainstream Jewish thinking in calling humankind to mend its ways and "not oppress the alien, orphan and the widow" (Jer 7:3–4) by our unjust actions. Jesus put his questioning followers in their place when they challenged him with "Lord, when did we see you hungry or thirsty, a stranger or naked, or in prison?' (Matt 25:44). Central to all the

17. Williams, *Essential Writings*.
18. Sachs, *End of Poverty*, 289.

Abrahamic faiths is their prohibition of unjust actions or those behaviors that condemn (or hold) others in poverty.

In similar fashion, we can note the Qu'ran's insistent teaching that humankind are *khalifa*, which means that they are guardians or stewards of the created order. *Khalifa* is often translated as "friend of Earth." This aligns with the Hebrew concept of personal stewardship for creation, which stems from the Genesis narratives through the prophetic utterances and the ministry of Jesus into New Testament teaching. In the Abrahamic faiths, "care for the Earth" as part of life as God's people is vital—in every sense.

The thinking of many pagans and other pantheists, ecologists, and "green" politicians share this understanding of both *khalifa* and "care for the earth." "As Schumacher told the world, Buddhist economics is about trying to live our lives in right relationship. If an action damages the web of life, we should turn and think again. If it sustains it, then all are blessed."[19] As a Christian educator, I affirm that these values are a necessary part of the trajectory of Christian discipleship. "If we want to respond to creation differently, with loving care for all that lives on earth, and if we aspire to be what were meant to be, that is co-creators, created in God's image, then we must realise that creation refers not only to our origins but our future as well."[20]

Small is beautiful

But none of us can undertake *oikos* envisioning alone. "Among sedentary communities, the family is the institution that has traditionally harboured the strongest ties."[21] Often in today's fractured and disparate nations, our family members can be living miles apart in different regions, even countries—so we need to utilize other groups. In our town-wide Green Party, we lend each other books about economics, social policy, political theory, practical activism, and food growing, as well as meeting for business or eating together. In our Anabaptist-Christian-oriented home group, we meet frequently to pray, to eat, read the Bible, listen to and learn from our group's understanding of discipleship issues, talking about books we have read. Together with our local friends, we often share meals and resources (vehicles, ladders, tools, books, etc.) as well as our surplus produce, favor-

19. McIntosh, *Rekindling Community*, 100.

20. Soelle and Cloyes, *To Work and to Love*, 163.

21. Dasgupta, *Economics*, 100.

ite recipes, and specialist cookware. Working together in small committed groups supports each of us to live fuller and Earth-friendly lives.

"Economists and statisticians find it useful to work with a more contemporary notion—the household—which is a smaller unit than the family. The household is usually taken to mean a unit of housekeeping or consumption. Its members eat meals together or eat meals that are derived from a common stock of food."[22] But I would argue that this understanding of "household" (*oikos*) limits the strength and interrelationships of the small, purpose-driven clan, group, or faith community. The small Nenet clans of interrelated herders (1) are an example of such economic "households," which challenge our Westernized notions. As are groups like our radical Christian home-group or our close circle of local friends—as explained above. Lest we forget, the very word *oikos* carries the implication of "the household." Our life together helps witness to our shared *oikos* vision.

City planners, denominational authorities, and evangelical pastors often talk of "economy of scale," wanting people to be part of bigger cities, schools, and housing projects or central congregations or mega-churches. But it is not just my experience (ecclesially and socially) but that of many others that the small radical group can change perceptions and lifestyles.[23]

> We want to supersize our fries, sodas and church buildings. But amid all the supersizing, many of us feel God is doing something new, something small and subtle. This thing Jesus called the kingdom of God is emerging across the globe in the most unexpected places, a gentle whisper amid the chaos. Little people with big dreams are reimagining the world. Little communities of ordinary radicals are committed to doing small things with great love.[24]

Whether I am harvesting my vegetables, making bread or soup to share, throwing a pot, paunching a shot rabbit, or leading a friend's burial service, I am very conscious of our connection with God's Earth: "ashes to ashes, dust to dust" (Eccl 12:7). Through the writings and work of the Scottish theologian Alastair McIntosh, I have learned much of human ecology, as well as its insistent demand to question how we live now. "Change that violates interconnectedness causes degradation, loss and extinction . . . . We need, first, to make community with the soil, to learn how to revere the Earth . . . second, we need to make community of human society . . . and

22. Ibid.

23. Banks and Banks, *Church Comes Home*.

24. Claiborne, *Irresistible Revolution*, 25.

third, but not least, we need to make community of the soul."[25] This book shares the same threefold thesis as McIntosh.

The canary in the coal mine

In the history of coal mining, caged canaries were taken down the pit. While the canaries sang, all was good. But when they gave out agitated sounds and died, the miners knew that toxic coal-gas was increasing and they had to escape to the surface, fresh air, and life itself.

Some years ago, I had been speaking forcefully on a national radio program about the fashionistas' regrettable demands for globally branded products. One generous listener sent me a book by the Canadian writer Naomi Klein, who was far more cogently strong in expressing those *shared* opinions about such branding.[26] Increasingly, I have found that Klein uses both her globally syndicated column and her secular Hebrew philosophy to inform an increasingly "Earth-friendly," zero-growth trajectory, appropriately questioning the Westernized status quo.[27] As I write, her latest book *This Changes Everything: Capitalism vs. The Climate* sits on my shelf, reminding me that others with different worldviews and faith backgrounds share the challenge and premise of this *oikos* book.

In the UK, we were once blessed with two particular magazines. *Resurgence* was a monthly focus upon comparative nonsectarian spirituality, while *The Ecologist* was vital to all of us seeking greater Earth-friendly lifestyles or habits. They united as a single magazine in fall 2012, under the guiding editorship of Satish Kumar, who is Indian by background, a former Jain monk, much influenced by Gandhi and Schumacher but now better known as a writer, international peace campaigner, and community activist. Shortly afterwards, Kumar produced another stimulating book, *Soil, Soul, Society: A New Trinity for Our Time*; he even explores the eco/*oikos* theme as part of his thesis. It echoes the threefold theme of the Scottish Quaker McIntosh and this book, in its challenge to its readers: "Care of the soil and the soul needs to be extended to include care for society"[28]—ecology, ecumeny, and economy, again.

25. McIntosh, *Soil and Soul*, 283–84.

26. Klein, *NO Logo*.

27. Klein, *Fences and Windows*.

28. Kumar, *Soil, Soul, Society*, 26.

Every year, the World Economic Forum takes place in Davos, Switzerland, where economists, politicians, and business moguls gather in their thousands for a week of high-level seminars and policy discussions. Alongside, the economic agenda run at least two parallel themes that inform the central agenda. Excitingly, in 2016 the parallel themes were robotics and "environmental science" (or ecology by another name!). Davos 2016 seriously recognized the economic threat of global warming and climate change for "time is short and the water rises." While Davos WEF 2016 was taking place, several of the international stock exchanges, including China's, dropped to (or significantly towards) "bear market" status.[29] During all this, the BBC repeatedly broadcast an interview with the aforementioned economist, Stiglitz, who maintained that the developed world "had had its warnings, both economically and environmentally . . . and had to change." Stiglitz referred positively to the work of his predecessors (e.g. Sachs, Daly) and the zero growth advocated by Piketty "and other green economists."

Ecologists have been singing out for generations, at last the warning songs of other people for the current life of the world are joining them. When secular Jewish Canadian columnist Naomi Klein, or retired UK chancellor Nigel Lawson (23) or the urbane Satish Kumar have global readerships for their questioning of societal norms and how they change, the songs have different melodies but the same insistent rhythm. Part of Daly and Cobb's vision for the world is as a single biosphere, where all species live together for the common good and the planet's healthy ecology: "The biospheric vision is richly inclusive and transformative of human perceptions. Once community with other living things is truly experienced and appreciated, aspects of our thinking and our way of life previously taken for granted become unacceptable. In short, it is in itself a religious vision."[30]

When community theologians like McIntosh, McFague, Soelle, or even myself bring our different radical theologies to bear, they are in concert together with the Earth-friendly life, crosscultural ministry, and alternative economic teaching of Jesus. When the martyrs of Daesh's violence really touch both Westernized hypocrisies and peaceable Muslims, the song of peace will sound over the drums of war and chorus the cries of the starving. When the multinationals and global politicians realize there are no new markets nor extra money and that land and natural resources

29. A "bear market" occurs when a particular stock exchange's index (e.g. Dow Jones) falls by 20 percent from its previous highest peak.

30. Daly and Cobb, *For the Common Good*, 377

are finite, the chorus of those green economists will be properly recognized. The canaries are singing . . . and thanks to Maya Angelou, we know why the caged bird sings.

What is vital is to respect and recognize the integrity and faith or philosophy of these many different people. They are not all the same and we serve the world poorly if we try to mix them up in some misguided syncretism or porridge. Each voice needs to be heard for *who* they are in the image of God. As Jonathan Sacks began another recent book, "Multiculturalism has run its course and it is time to move on."[31] His vision for recreating society relied upon respect, integrity, and vitality of faith rather than some forms of increasingly diluted liberal democracy or advancing secular tolerance, to protect the common skin we all share.

A common skin?

I was once offered a barren and polluted community garden (UK=allotment), where already exhausted topsoil had been put on a former rubbish heap. It was polluted beyond belief—this small crust of the earth was desiccated and almost blue with oil stains. It was good for nothing, because its previous users had repeatedly abused it. The earth only has one skin and, once destroyed, it cannot be redeemed without huge sacrifice and change.

As part of a world population, we each share this planet's common skin and whether it is the Amazon basin, the African dust bowls, or my potential allotment, we cannot afford socially and economically any further ecological destruction of that which we share. All the Abrahamic faiths call for human justice in the name of their God, whatever race or wealth we own. The common skin we share calls us to find our life as world citizens, together. We must learn to sing from the same hymn-sheet and walk with those who "have been to the mountaintop."[32]

Pope Francis said, "We need to strengthen the conviction that we are one single human family. There are no frontiers or barriers, political or social, behind which we can hide, still less is there room for the globalization of indifference."[33] On that note, even this radical Protestant can believe the Pope may on occasions be infallible! The fact is that we all share a common

---

31. Sacks, *Home We Build Together*.

32. Referring to the visionary address given by Dr. Martin Luther King Jr., in Memphis, on April 3, 1968—the day before his assassination.

33. Francis, *Laudato Si'*, para. 52, 29.

skin, whatever our race, poverty or wealth, and gender, and it is only by moving in a commonly shared direction that humankind can have forward movement—and therefore a future.

Epilogue

As every transatlantic traveler knows, the tastes of British and US chocolate are different. When the multinational Kraft (food conglomerate) took over the very British Cadbury chocolate firm, some brands of that chocolate were altered to make them more globally acceptable. The devolved parent company of Cadbury also moved its taxation totally offshore, thus depriving the British exchequer of billions of pounds of taxation.

In this brave new world, we must recognize three things:

1. Products will be altered, and regional tastes, even needs, ignored to meet the global market: the new community is the world.

2. Multinationals will quite legally diminish their tax liabilities by shifting them to tax havens and offsetting profits against losses all across the globe, further diminishing what they will pay their workers.

3. Individual nations can no longer be self-sufficient but must recognize their own place as a cog in global machinations.

We must *now* live as part of God's global household—the *oikos* presumption—in every way. This will include the globally responsible diet that we *should* have, the need to accept lifestyle constraints as climate change increases, and ensuring that our national energy production and personal consumption diminishes. Neither climate change nor the changing economic world order will allow traditional western nations to buy their way out of trouble.

As I was researching this book, Jeffrey Sachs, the international economist and adviser to both the UN and US presidents, published a new book, *The Age of Sustainable Development*. I rejoiced to read its thesis that sustainability can and will only occur when three factors come together: economy, ecology, and social cohesion (ecumeny, by another name). Sachs is an academic, writing accordingly, but his book's 500-plus pages are encouragingly both eminently readable and yield many quotes per page. I encourage you to read it, should you wish to explore the threefold *oikos* theme from the economic perspective.

In reading this book, you will have realized that the necessary change must be accomplished by new patterns of integration which do not threaten, but allow decentralization of government and localization of economies. "There is a clear need for integration that does not threaten people's need to develop in their own way. The suspicion of a dragooned assimilation will always exist until a more creative consensus emerges on what society should aim for. Religion is inevitably part of that process."[1]

Virtually every nation of the world is influenced by one or more of the Abrahamic faiths. At the heart of each of their "codes" of belief is the desire for peace. To risk the accusation of proof-texting, the successive teaching of "Thou shalt not kill" (Exod 20:13), Jesus' teaching of "Turn the other cheek" (Matt 5:39 and Q. 5:32) point towards this. However, both Jewish and Islamic scholars and commentators argue about the contexts and caveats applicable to their teachings. Are these universal or are the apostate/nonbeliever exempt and can therefore be killed? "The majority of people living on our planet profess to be believers. This should spur religions to dialogue among themselves for the sake of protecting nature, defending the poor, and building networks of respect and fraternity."[2] If the current earthly leader of the global Roman Catholic community can advocate this, only the bigoted Protestant Christian, unthinking Jewish rabbi, or thoughtless imam will not seek to heed and promote that common call for the sake of the world in the name of the God in whom we all believe.

When I was a teenager, my father taught in one of the international colleges in Selly Oak, Birmingham, UK. I spent a couple of happy summers acting as a tour guide for our many north American visitors. After a day leading one such family around the William Shakespeare properties, in nearby Stratford-upon-Avon, they gave me several gifts, including some US dollars; real ones, this time "for your first trip to the States." They also gave me a postcard, with the environmental eulogy of Chief Seattle printed upon it. That postcard traveled across all my student pinboards, then seminary

---

1. Newbigin, Sanneh, and Taylor, *Faith and Power*, 103

2. Francis, *Laudato Si'*, para. 201, 96.

until it finally fell apart but its words are seared into my head and heart: "Every part of the earth is sacred to my people . . . our God is also your God: the earth is precious to him and to harm the world is to heap contempt upon its creator . . . this we know; the earth does not belong to man, man belongs to the earth."

Soon afterwards I began learning biblical Hebrew, including the fact that the name of Adam, the representative human in the Genesis creation allegory, is drawn from *adamah*, meaning "earth" or "ground." So in my faith's thinking that representative man, Adam is indeed a "child of the earth"; Chief Seattle's animist reflections coincide with that of Judeo-Christian orthodoxy. Shared thinking and religious dialogue are possible.

We only have this one planet. We share it whether it is a garden or a wasteland—be that agriculturally, economically, metaphorically, or socially. How we share life in this garden of captives is a matter of human choice and conscience—whether faith-based or profit-driven.

Thus began the thinking and philosophy behind my lifetime's *oikos* journey via many radical Christian traditions and communities, green politics and deeper "Earth-friendly" discipleship. As my research skills were honed, I discovered how often Chief Seattle's words had been redacted to suit the whims of those promoting them in different formats. Likewise, the world's peoples are being corralled away from those who might challenge the hegemonies and profits of "the suit" and the vested interests of the transnationals.

Part of that tactic is to create diversionary false dichotomies, whether between science and spirituality, or ensuring enmities between faith groups. It is far more likely to be the Western capitalist or Russian or Chinese oligarch who financially profits from the sale of armaments to the Islamist (and other) terrorists to strike against the consumerist West, than a needy developing world peasant. Our criteria for true reflection must be holistic and see past the screens erected by those who want to destroy our sightlines. "If you judge a person by how well he plays pool, Mozart won't pass scrutiny, but the fault is in your lens."[3]

The lens of our worldview will determine how much of God's *oikos* vision we accept. We are also held captive by the narrowness of the lens we hold dear to.

For both individuals and nations, an insular attitude will potentially lead to greater isolation. Choices have to be made. Nations like Vietnam,

3. Chopra and Mlodinow, *War of the Worldviews*, 302.

with a tourist-driven, currency-earning economy and agricultural self-sustaining lifestyle have adopted a simple Earth-friendly, cooperative political vision.[4] South Korea, exemplified by the transnational Hyundai corporation, demonstrate a profit-driven industrial, capitalist vision, which must change recognizably.[5] The nations traditionally known as being Westernized have to wrestle with the *oikos* vision to determine the holism of their ongoing political vision and national lifestyle, and what *can* be permissible as a proportionate sharing of earth's resources "for the common good." Faith communities have an overwhelming contribution to offer in every nation and neighborhood in reshaping the Westernized, growth-economy nations in choosing a holistic future *oikos* pattern and philosophy "for the common good."

The connections need to be made . . . and that will begin with individuals. We must applaud the example of the newly elected Mayor of London in 2016, Sadiq Khan, a Muslim, who chose the Anglican Southwark Cathedral for his formal acceptance speech and induction to office. On that occasion, he embraced Christian leaders, Jewish rabbis, and Muslim imams while calling on *all* Londoners to work together, welcome visitors and refugees, and build new homes and communities "for the common good."[6]

Likewise, increasing but measured federalization, as well as decentralization, will need to occur if we are really to make an impact together to produce a realistic downshift in the usage of world resources, and to establish peaceable cooperation between nations and new patterns of economic life. We only need to look at the European Union that has arisen from the ashes and poverty of postwar Europe, and the wise insights of a Dutch social commentator to realize this: "The foundations upon which the EU is built, are now an increasing reality in the daily life of each citizen. It is no longer the pioneers, the statesmen or the nations which shore up the Union, it is above all that immense warp and weft of the businesses, cities and people, that slowly-developed self-evident European existence that will have to weather that storm."[7]

I see myself far more as European or a world citizen than as an Englander. Foolishly, the English electorate voted to leave the EU, stranding our partner nations of Scotland and Northern Ireland, whose voters had

4. Lien and Sharrock, *Descending Dragon.*

5. Eichengreen et al., *Korean Economy.*

6. May 6, 2016.

7. Mak, *In Europe,* 822.

democratically chosen to stay in, isolating and potentially fragmenting the UK and its future while European nations and the economic "unions" of ASEAN (Asia), MERCOSUR (South America) and the African Union looked on and continue to learn what isolation really means.

And now it is your turn. "In his book *The Future of Life*, the famed biologist, E. O. Wilson . . . calls Homo Sapiens 'the serial killer of the biosphere'. Global warming. The melting of the polar ice-caps. The poisoning of the seas and skies. The fires burning through the Amazon. Millions of us, driving our children to school, driving to the grocery, driving to work."[8] Having read this book, check off anything on that short list which applies to you or your family, through your lifestyle, learning, and consumerism. What changes do you need to make?

Those Nenet caribou herders believed they would live in isolation but GazProm and the rest of us will not let them. Many Alaskan homesteaders believed they had a self-sustaining lifestyle until the *Exxon Valdez* changed all that. The Vietnamese believed they had a self-sustaining politic until French colonialists then Coca-Cola–bearing GIs tried to change all that.

Within the last ten years, I spent some nights volunteering in a homeless shelter in a European capital where many were homeless migrants earning sub-legal wages because "the suit" needed their labor. I eat a whole range of store-bought world foods alongside what I *choose* to grow on rain-watered land close to my home—and as you have time to read this book, I expect that you have opportunity to choose your diet, too. Today, one in seven of the world's population will have lived on less than US$1 and may be homeless and not just hungry but starving. We live in an inequitable world where we are not working fast enough to redress matters as God intends. This is life in our garden of captives, where we either ignore or are easily distracted from making the *oikos* connections.

"Learning to live (much more) simply so that others may simply live" can no longer be only a theologian's mantra but is a global necessity. Some abiding memories of my earlier life involve sharing food in stressed neighborhoods or peasant communities, listening to stories of adversity and receiving hospitality of hard-gotten victuals. I did not return easily to comfortable motels after such experiences, often rather sleeping under a meager blanket on the hard earth or on a cabin cot. As I then turned to sleep, without light to read or opportunity to phone home, I recalled the promises of God, the life and words of Jesus, and some of his present-day

8. French, *Zoo Story*, 235.

followers with whom I share understandings. "The roots of ecology, economics and ecumenism are all in *oikos*: with the right management of the [global] household—respect for the integrity of nature and equitable sharing of resources—all can be included at the dinner table."[9] There may be no table, just a mealie pot or trapper's stew or a trash-can grill in a downtown backlot, but God's *oikos* is for all people, not just "the suit" and those of us blessed to be born in nations of plenty.

But we are the ones who must ensure that things change. Begin with *oikos* today . . . yet know it will take much, both materially and committedly, from us and time before the world cries *Amen*. Our task is to make sure the world says *Amen* to God's *oikos* vision. So be it!

9. McFague, *Life Abundant*, 36.

Bibliography

Abou El Fadl, Khaled. *The Great Theft: Wrestling Islam from the Extremists*. San Francisco: HarperCollins, 2007.

Akhtar, Shabbir. *The Light in the Enlightenment: Christianity and the Secular Heritage*. London: Grey Seal, 1990.

Aristophanes. "The Acharnians." In *Aristophanes Plays 1* 1–60. Oxford: Berg 3PL, 1993.

Armstrong, Karen. *The Battle for God: Fundamentalism in Judaism, Christianity and Islam*. London: HarperCollins, 2001.

———. *Islam: A Short History*. Abergavenny, Wales: Phoenix, 2001.

Arthus-Bertrand, Yann. *2 Degrees Too High: Understanding the Copenhagen Summit*. New York: Harry N. Abrams, 2009.

Bakke, Ray. *The Urban Christian*. Leicester: Inter-Varsity, 1987.

Bang, Jan Martin. *Ecovillages: A Practical Guide to Sustainable Communities*. Edinburgh: Floris, 2005.

Banks, Robert, and Julia Banks. *The Church Comes Home*. Peabody, MA: Hendrickson, 1998.

Barber, Benjamin R. *Jihad v. McWorld*. London: Corgi, 2003.

Bauckham, Richard. *Bible and Ecology: Rediscovery of the Community of Creation*. London: Darton, Longman & Todd, 2010.

Berners-Lee, Mike. *How Bad are Bananas: The Carbon Footprint of Everything*. London: Profile, 2010.

Berners-Lee, Mike, and Duncan Clark. *The Burning Question: We Can't Burn Half the World's Oil, Coal and Gas. So How Do We Quit?* London: Profile, 2013.

Berry, Wendell. *The Art of the Commonplace: The Agrarian Essays of Wendell Berry*. Washington, DC: Counterpoint, 2002.

Boff, Leonardo, and Virgil Elizondo. *Ecology and Poverty: Cry of the Earth, Cry of the Poor*. Maryknoll, NY: Orbis, 1995.

Bowen, E. G. *Saints, Seaways and Settlements*. London: Unwin, 1969.

Bradley, Ian. *God is Green: Ecology for Christians*. London: Doubleday, 1992.

Brandt, Willy, ed. *North-South: A Program for Survival*. Boston: MIT Press, 1990.

Brueggemann, Walter. *The Land*. Minneapolis: Fortress, 2002.

———. *Living toward a Vision*. New York: United Church, 1982.

Carson, Rachel. *Silent Spring*. London: Penguin, 1965.

Chopra, Deepak, and Leonard Mlodinow. *War of the Worldviews: Where Science and Spirituality Meet—And Do Not.* New York: Three Rivers, 2012.

Chryssavgis, John, and Bruce V. Foltz, eds. *Toward an Ecology of Transfiguration: Orthodox Christian Perspectives on Environment, Nature, and Creation. Orthodox Christianity and Contemporary Thought.* New York: Fordham University Press, 2013.

Claiborne, Shane. *Irresistible Revolution: Living as an Ordinary Radical.* Grand Rapids: Zondervan, 2006.

Clark, Kelly James. *Abraham's Children: Liberty and Tolerance in an Age of Religious Conflict.* New Haven: Yale University Press, 2012.

Collis, John Stewart. *Down to Earth.* London: Jonathan Cape, 1947.

———. *The Vision of Glory: The Extraordinary Nature of the Ordinary.* London: Charles Knight, 1972.

Costanza, Robert, ed. *An Introduction to Ecological Economics.* Boca Raton, FL: St. Lucie, 1997.

Cragg, Gerald R. *The Church in an Age of Reason, 1648–1789.* London: Penguin, 1990.

da Mosto, Francesco, *Francesco's Venice: the Dramatic History of the World's Most Beautiful City.* London: BBC, 2004.

Daly, Herman E. *Beyond Growth: The Economics of Sustainable Development.* Boston: Beacon, 1996.

Daly, Herman E., and John B Cobb, Jr. *For the Common Good: Redirecting the Economy toward Community, the Environment, and a Sustainable Future.* Boston: Beacon, 1994.

Dasgupta, Partha. *Economics: A Very Short Introduction.* Oxford: Oxford University Press, 2007.

Dawkins, Richard. *The God Delusion.* Boston: Houghton Mifflin, 2006.

Deane-Drummond, Celia. *Eco-Theology.* London: Darton, Longman and Todd, 2008.

Dick, Philip K. *Do Androids Dream of Electric Sheep?* London: Gollancz, 2010.

Dietz, Rob, and Dan O'Neill. *Enough is Enough: Building a Sustainable Economy in a World of Finite Resources.* London: Routledge, 2013.

Duiker, William J. *Ho Chi Minh: A Life.* New York: Hyperion, 2000.

Eichengreen, Barry, Wonhyuk Lim, Yung Chul Park, and Dwight H. Perkins. *The Korean Economy: From a Miraculous Past to a Sustainable Future.* Cambridge, MA: Harvard University Press, 2015.

Emmott, Stephen. *Ten Billion.* London: Penguin, 2013.

Engels, Friedrich, and David McLellan. *The Condition of the Working Class in England.* Oxford: Oxford World's Classics, 2009.

Felber, Christian. *Change Everything: Economics for the Common Good.* London: Zed, 2015.

Fenby, Jonathan. *The Penguin History of Modern China: The Fall and Rise of a Great Power, 1850 to the Present.* London: Penguin, 2013.

Fernando, Leonard, and G. Sauch-Gispert. *Christianity in India: Two Thousand Years of Faith.* Kolkata: Viking, 2004.

Foreman, Amanda. *The World Made by Women: A History of Women from the Dawn of Civilization.* London: Allen Lane, 2016.

Forsyth, Frederick. *The Outsider.* London: Bantam, 2015.

Fox, Matthew. *Original Blessing: Primer in Creation Spirituality.* San Francisco: Bear, 1983.

Francis. *Laudato Si': On Care for Our Common Home.* London: Catholic Truth Society, 2015.

Francis, Andrew. *Anabaptism: Radical Christianity*. Bristol: Antioch, 2010.

———. *Dorothee Soelle: Life and Work*. Bristol: Imagier, 2014.

———. *Earth, Air, Fire, Water*. Bristol: Kettle Press Poetry, 2015.

———. *Hospitality and Community after Christendom*. Milton Keynes: Paternoster, 2012.

———. *Shalom: The Jesus Manifesto*. Milton Keynes, UK: Paternoster, 2016.

———. *What in God's Name are You Eating?* Eugene, OR: Cascade, 2014.

Francis, Andrew, ed. *Foxes Have Holes: Christian Reflections upon Britain's Housing Need*. London: Ekklesia, 2016.

French, Thomas. *Zoo Story: Life in the Garden of Captives*. New York: Hyperion, 2010.

Fretheim, Terence E. *Abraham: Trials of Family and Faith. Studies on Personalities of the Old Testament*. Columbia: South Carolina University Press, 2007.

Friesen, Duane K. *Artists, Citizens, Philosophers*. Scottdale, PA: Herald, 2000.

Galbraith, J. K. *The Affluent Society*. London: Penguin, 1999.

———. *American Capitalism: The Concept of Countervailing Power*. London: Hamish Hamilton, 1964.

Gandhi, M. K. *The Story of My Experiments with Truth*. London: Phoenix, 1949.

Gill, Athol. *Life on the Road*. Scottdale, PA: Herald, 1992.

Gonzales-Balado, José Luis. *The Story of Taizé*. London: Mowbray, 1988.

Goodall, Chris. *Ten Technologies to Fix Energy and Climate*. London: Profile, 2009.

Gore, Al. *An Inconvenient Truth: The Planetary Emergency of Global Warming and What We Can Do About It*. London: Bloomsbury, 2006.

Granberg-Michaelson, Wesley, ed. *Tending the Earth: Essays on the Gospel and the Earth*. Grand Rapids: Eerdmans, 1987.

Gregorios, Paulos Mar. "New Testament Foundations for Understanding Creation." In *Tending the Earth: Essays on the Gospel and the Earth*, edited by Wesley Granberg-Michaelson, 83–92. Grand Rapids: Eerdmans, 1987.

Hackett, Steven C. *Environmental and Natural Resources Economics: Theory, Policy and the Sustainable Society*. Armonk: M. C. Sharpe, 1998.

Harari, Yuval Noah. *Homo Sapiens: A Brief History of Humankind*. New York: Vintage, 2015.

Hart, Michael. *A Trading Nation: Canadian Trade Policy from Colonialism to Globalization. Canada and International relations*. Vancouver, BC: University of British Columbia Press, 2003.

Hauerwas, Stanley, and William Willimon. *Resident Aliens: Life in the Christian Colony*. Nashville: Abingdon, 1989.

Hay, Donald A., and Alan Kreider, eds. *Christianity and the Culture of Economics*. Cardiff: University of Wales Press, 2001.

Hebden, Keith. *Seeking Justice: The Radical Compassion of Jesus*. Winchester: Circle, 2013.

Herbert, Nick. *Quantum Reality: Beyond the New Physics*. New York: Doubleday, 1985.

Hodson, Martin and Margot. "Climate Justice." In *Carnival Kingdom: Biblical Justice for Global Communities*, edited by Marijke Hoek, et al., 125–44. Gloucester: Wide Margin, 2013.

Hoek, Marijke, Jonathan Ingleby, Andy Kingston-Smith and Carol Kingston-Smith, eds. *Carnival Kingdom: Biblical Justice for Global Communities*. Gloucester: Wide Margin, 2013.

Hosseini, Khaled. *A Thousand Splendid Suns*. London: Bloomsbury, 2008.

Houllebecq, Michel. *Platform*. London: Heinemann, 2002.

Jackson, Tim. *Prosperity without Growth: Economics for a Crowded Planet*. London: Routledge, 2011.

Jacques, Martin. *When China Rules the World: The End of the Western World and the Birth of a New Global Order*. London: Penguin, 2012.

Jamal, Mahmood. *Islamic Mystical Poetry: Sufi Verse: From the Early Mystics to Rumi*. London: Penguin, 2009.

Juniper, Tony. *Saving Planet Earth*. London: BBC/HarperCollins, 2007.

Karnow, Stanley. *Vietnam*. London: Penguin, 1991.

Keay, John. *The Honourable Company: A History of the English East India Company*. London: HarperCollins, 1993.

Keynes, John Maynard. *The Essential Keynes*. London: Penguin Classics, 2015.

Kingston-Smith, Andy. "Migrants, Justice and Border Lives." In *Carnival Kingdom: Biblical Justice for Global Communities*, edited by Marijke Hoek et al., 101–23. Gloucester: Wide Margin, 2013.

Kirby, David. *Death at Sea World*. New York: St. Martin's Griffin, 2013.

Klein, Naomi. *Fences and Windows: Dispatches from the Frontline of the Globalisation Debate*. London: Flamingo, 2010.

———. *NO Logo: Taking Aim at the Brand Bullies*. London: Fourth Estate, 2010.

———. *This Changes Everything: Capitalism vs. the Climate*. London: Penguin, 2015.

Kraybill, Donald B. "Amish Economics: The Interface of Religious Values and Economic Interests." In *Christianity and the Culture of Economics*, edited by Donald A. Hay and Alan Kreider, 76-90. Cardiff: University of Wales Press, 2001.

Kraybill, Donald, and Steven M. Nolt. *Amish Enterprise*. Baltimore: Johns Hopkins University Press, 1995.

Kreider, Alan. *Origin of Christendom in the West*. New York: Continuum, 2001.

———. *The Patient Ferment of the Early Church: The Improbable Rise of Christianity in the Roman Empire*. Grand Rapids: Baker, 2016.

Kropotkin, Peter. *The Conquest of Bread*. Mineola, NY: Dover, 2011.

———. *Fields, Factories and Workshops*. Eastford, CT: Martino, 2014.

———. *Mutual Aid: a Factor in Evolution*. New York: Cosimo, 2009.

Kumar, Satish. *Soil, Soul, Society: A New Trinity for Our Time*. Lewes, UK: Leaping Hare, 2013.

Kwarteng, Kwasi. *War and Gold: A Five-Hundred-Year History of Empires, Adventures and Debt*. London: Bloomsbury, 2014.

Lawson, Nigel. *The View from Number 1*. London: Bantam, 1992.

Leakey, Richard. *The Origin of Humankind*. London: Weidenfield & Nicholson, 1994.

Lien, Vu Hong, and Peter D. Sharrock. *Descending Dragon, Rising Tiger: A History of Vietnam*. London: Reaktion, 2014.

Lippard, Lucy. *Pop Art*. London: Thames & Hudson, 1967.

Longacre, Doris Janzen. *Living More with Less*. Scottdale, PA: Herald, 2010.

Lovelock, James. *Gaia: A New Look at Life on Earth*. Oxford: Oxford University Press, 1979.

———. *The Vanishing Face of Gaia: A Final Warning: Enjoy It While You Can*. London: Allen Lane, 2009.

Lynas, Mark. *Six Degrees: Our Future on a Hotter Planet*. London: Harper, 2008.

MacAskill, William. *Doing Good Better: Effective Altruism and a Radical New Way to Make a Difference*. London: Guardian Faber, 2015.

MacLeod, George. *Only One Way Left*. Glasgow: Iona Community, 1956.

Madron, Roy, and John Jopling. *Gaian Democracies*. Totnes, UK: Green Books/ Schumacher Briefings, 2003.

Mak, Geert. *In Europe: Travels through the Twentieth Century*. London: Vintage, 2008.

Marshall, Alfred. *Principles of Economics*. New York: Cosimo, 2009.

Marx, Karl. *Capital: Critique of Political Economy*. London: Penguin, 1992.

———. *Grundrisse: Foundations of the Critique of a Political Economy*. London: Penguin, 1993.

Marx, Karl, and Friedrich Engels. *The Communist Manifesto*. London: Penguin, 2004.

Masood, Ehsan. *Science and Islam—a History*. London: Icon, 2009.

McFague, Sallie. *Life Abundant: Re-thinking Theology and Economy for a Planet in Peril*. Minneapolis: Fortress, 2000.

———. *A New Climate for Theology: God, the World and Global Warming*. Minneapolis: Fortress, 2008.

McGregor, Alisdair, Cole Roberts, and Fiona Cousins. *Two Degrees: The Built Environment and Our Changing Climate*. London: Routledge, 2012.

McIntosh, Alastair. *Rekindling Community*. Totnes, UK: Green Books/Schumacher Society, 2008.

———. *Soil and Soul*. London: Aurum, 2001.

Merton, Thomas. *Contemplation in a World of Action*. Notre Dame, IN: University of Notre Dame Press, 1999.

Meyer, Art, and Jocele Meyer. *Earthkeepers: Environmental Perspectives on Hunger, Poverty and Justice*. Scottdale, PA: Herald, 1991.

Monbiot, George, *Feral: Rewilding the Land, the Sea and Human Life*. London: Penguin, 2014.

———. *Heat: How We Can Stop the Planet Burning*. London: Penguin, 2007.

Moules, Noel. *Fingerprints of Fire, Footprints of Peace*. Washington, DC: O Books, 2012.

Murray, Stuart. *Beyond Tithing*. Milton Keynes, UK: Paternoster, 2002.

———. *The Challenge of the City: A Biblical View*. Tonbridge, UK: Sovereign World, 1993.

———. *Post-Christendom: Church and Mission in a Strange New World*. Milton Keynes, UK: Paternoster, 2004.

Newbigin, Lesslie, Lamin Sanneh, and Jenny Taylor. *Faith and Power: Christianity and Islam in "Secular" Britain*. Eugene, OR: Wipf and Stock, 1998.

Obama, Barack. *The Audacity of Hope*. New York: Three Rivers, 2006.

Parfitt, Tudor, and Yehuda Nini, eds. *Israel and Ishmael: Studies in Muslim-Jewish Relations*. London: St Martin's, 2000.

Pearse, Meic. *Age of Reason: From the Wars of Religion to the French Revolution, 1570– 1789*. Tunbridge Wells, UK: Monarch, 2007.

Peters, F. E. *The Children of Abraham: Judaism, Christianity, Islam*. Princeton, NJ: Princeton University Press, 2006.

Pickthall, Mohammed Marmaduke. *The Meaning of the Glorious Koran: An Explanatory Translation*. Scarborough, CA: Mentor, 1980.

Piketty, Thomas. *Capital in the Twenty First Century*. Cambridge, MA: Harvard University Press, 2013.

Pohl, Christine. *Making Room*. Grand Rapids: Eerdmans, 1999.

Popper, Nathaniel. *Digital Gold: The Untold Story of Bitcoin*. New York / London: Penguin, 2016.

Porritt, Jonathan. *Seeing Green: The Politics of Ecology Explained*. Oxford: Wiley-Blackwell, 1984.

Putnam, Robert D. *Bowling Alone.* New York: Simon & Schuster, 2001.

———. *Our Kids: The American Dream in Crisis.* New York: Simon & Schuster, 2015.

———. *Integrating Ecofeminism, Globalisation and World Religions.* Lanham: Rowman & Littlefield, 2004.

Ramon (Brother). *Franciscan Spirituality: Following St Francis Today.* London: SPCK, 1994.

Reynolds, Kevin, dir. *Robin Hood: Prince of Thieves.* Burbank, CA: Warner Brothers Entertainment, 1991.

Rice, David Talbot. *Islamic Art.* London: Thames & Hudson, 1975.

Rieger, Joerg, ed. *Liberating the Future: God, Mammon and Theology.* Minneapolis: Augsberg Fortress, 1998.

Roeg, Nicholas, dir. *Don't Look Now.* DVD. Orig. released 1973. Hollywood: Paramount Home Media Distribution, 2002.

Ruether, Rosemary Radford. *Gaia and God: An Ecofeminist Theology of Earth Healing.* London: SCM, 1992.

Rushdie, Salman. *The Satanic Verses.* London: Vintage, 1998.

Sachs, Jeffrey. *The Age of Sustainable Development.* New York: Columbia University Press, 2015.

———. *Commonwealth: Economics for a Crowded Planet.* New York: Allen Lane, 2008.

———. *The End of Poverty.* New York: Penguin, 2005.

Sacks, Jonathan. *The Dignity of Difference.* London: Continuum International, 2002.

———. *The Home We Build Together: Re-creating Society.* London: Continuum, 2009.

———. *Not in God's Name: Confronting Religious Violence.* London: Hodder & Stoughton, 2015.

Sardar, Ziauddin, and Merryl Wyn Davies. *Distorted Imagination: Lessons from the Rushdie Affair.* London: Grey Seal, 1990.

Sawtell, Roger. "Co-operatives: Regenerating Business in the Twenty-First Century." In *Christianity and the Culture of Economics*, edited by Donald A. Hay and Alan Kreider, 52–75. Cardiff: University of Wales Press, 2001.

Schumacher, E. F. *A Guide for the Perplexed.* London: Vintage, 1995.

———. *Small is Beautiful: A Study of Economics as if People Matter.* London: Abacus, 1973.

Scott Cato, Molly. *Environment and Economy.* London: Routledge, 2011.

———. *Green Economics: An Introduction to Theory, Policy and Practice.* London: Routledge, 2008.

———. "Turning the World Upside Down." In *Carnival Kingdom: Biblical Justice for Global Communities*, edited by Marijke Hoek et al., 43–62. Gloucester: Wide Margin, 2013.

Shanks, Norman. *IONA: God's Energy—the Spirituality and Vision of the Iona Community.* London: Hodder & Stoughton, 1999.

Smith, Adam. *The Wealth of Nations.* London: Penguin 1970.

Soelle, Dorothee. *Celebrating Resistance.* London: Mowbray, 1993.

———. *Theology for Sceptics.* London: Mowbray, 1995.

———. *Thinking about God: An Introduction to Theology.* London: SCM, 1990.

Soelle, Dorothee, with Shirley Cloyes. *To Work and to Love: A Theology of Creation.* Philadelphia: Fortress, 1984.

Spink, Kathryn. *A Universal Heart: The Life and Vision of Brother Roger of Taizé.* London: SPCK, 2005.

Steinbeck, John. *The Grapes of Wrath*. London: Heinemann, 1939.

Stiglitz, Joseph. *Making Globalisation Work*. New York: W. W. Norton, 2006.

———. *The Price of Inequality: How Today's Divided Society Endangers our Future*. New York: W. W. Norton, 2012.

———. *The Stiglitz Report: Reforming the International Money and Financial Systems in the Wake of the Global Crisis*. London: New, 2010.

Stringer, Chris, and Robin McKie. *African Exodus: The Origins of Modern Humanity*. London: Pimlico, 1997.

Swaminathan, M. S. *Science and Sustainable Food Security: Selected Papers of M S Swaminathan*. Chennai, IN: World Scientific, 2010.

Taylor, John V. *Enough is Enough*. London: SCM-Canterbury, 1975.

Thomson, E. P. *The Making of the English Working Class*. London: Penguin, 1968.

Thoreau, Henry David. *Walden and Other Writings*. New York: Bantam, 1980.

Varoufakis, Yanis. *The Global Minotaur: America, Europe and the Future of the World Economy*. London: Zed, 2013.

Vincent, John. *Into the City*. London: Epworth, 1982.

Walker, Andrew, ed. *Spirituality in the City*. London: SPCK, 2005.

Walsh, John, and Robert Gannon. *Time is Short and the Water Rises*. New York: E. P. Dutton, 1967.

Weber, Max. *The Protestant Ethic and the Spirit of Capitalism*. London: Routledge, 2008.

Werner, Sarah. "Peace and Agriculture: Local Food in a Mennonite Context." *Anabaptist Witness* 2 (2015) 69–85.

Williams, Charles S. *Essential Writings in Spirituality and Theology*. Lanham, MD: Cowley, 1994.

Williams, Rowan. *Faith in the Public Square*. London: Bloomsbury Continuum, 2015.

———. "Urbanisation, the Christian Church and the Human Project." In *Spirituality in the City*, edited by Andrew Walker, 15–26. London: SPCK, 2005.

Wirzba, Norman. *The Paradise of God: Renewing Religion in an Ecological Age*. New York: Oxford, 2003.

Woodin, Michael, and Caroline Lucas. *Green Alternatives to Globalisation: A Manifesto*. London: Pluto, 2004.

Woolley, Helen. *Urban Open Spaces*. Oxford: Taylor & Francis/Routledge, 2003.

Wright, Peter. *Spycatcher: The Candid Autobiography of a Senior Intelligence Officer*. Sydney: Heinemann, 1987.

Young, Raymond. *Building Home, Building Hope*. Edinburgh: Church of Scotland, 2010.

Lightning Source UK Ltd.
Milton Keynes UK
UKOW03f2349250517
302049UK00002B/185/P